T5-AXO-071

PLACE IN RETURN BOX to remove this checkout from your record.
TO AVOID FINES return on or before date due.

DATE DUE	DATE DUE

MAYOR
IN
PRISON

Karuga Wandai

East African Educational Publishers
NAIROBI

Published by
East African Educational Publishers
Mpaka Road/Woodvale Grove, Westlands
P.O. BOX 45314
Nairobi

ISBN 9966-46-462-X

Printed by
General Printers Ltd.
Homa Bay Road
P.O. Box 18001
Nairobi
G9985

To my wife AGNES WACHERA and our children NJERI, IRUNGU, MUTHONI, KANYORO and WAIRIMU, who suffered great difficulties during my imprisonment.

To my mother NJERI KARUGA and my sister WAIRIMU GICHUHI whose continuous love sustained me in Kamiti Prison.

To friends and relatives who did everything they could for my release and suffered with me during that difficult time.

Finally, to justices PLATT, GACHUHI, the late NYARANGI, and to all others like them who are committed to JUSTICE and FAIRNESS.

Chapter One

HUMBLE BEGINNINGS

I was born Wandai in 1945 at a place called "Majengo" in what is now Karung'e Sub-location of Kangema Division in Murang'a District. I was the last child of my mother Lucy Njeri. I had two elder sisters Nelias Wanjiru and Millicent Wairimu. My father Karuga Kiiru died in 1944 at the age of 62. Hence, I never saw him.

My father had three wives namely, Waitherero or Wangari the eldest wife, Waiyego and my mother the youngest wife Waiyego had three sons namely Charagu, Jotham Kiiru and Mukumu and only one daughter Wairimu. Apart from his three wives, my father had taken over two other wives of his deceased step brother. He lived with them as his wives and maintained them as well as their children. The names of those wives were Gachiru and Wangari. When my father died, he was buried at Kaharu near the place of my birth.

My mother was born about 1910. She was the only daughter of my grandfather Wandai, a very respected and wealthy person. She married my father in 1930 at the age of about 20. She had never attended school.

I do not know exactly when I was born although unofficially I celebrate my birthday on 15th May. The year however was 1945. This I know exactly because other boys and girls from educated families who were born at the same time as me were registered as having been born then. The identification card I got in 1967 states I was born in 1948. The officer who was registering us simply estimated our ages.

When I told him the year of my birth was 1945 he didn't believe me.

My sister Wairimu whose job was to baby-sit me tells that I almost died in infancy. In fact at one time I fell so sick that my mother gave up on my life. She must have believed she was going to lose me as she had lost another child named after my paternal grandfather Kiiru. I was abandoned behind our granary where rubbish was normally heaped, to await certain death. When my mother went to the garden, Wairimu ran to where I was abandoned and found that I was still breathing. She retrieved me, kept me in her bed, prepared porridge for me and generally nursed me. When I had recovered, she informed my mother that I was alright. My mother could not believe it. My sister always boasts about how she saved me while my mother never likes to hear the story. Naturally, I respect Wairimu very much because I owe my life to her. We are very fond of each other. My mother too is a great friend of mine.

As far as I can remember, I grew up like any other Kikuyu boy of my time. I started tending cows and goats at an early age in the company of bigger boys. This was a lot of fun because when we drove the animals to the river, we usually witnessed the spectacle of bull-fighting. The older boys would order us to throw soil between the bulls' heads so as to stop the fighting. Apart from watching bull fights, we would also swim in river Godo. While swimming, we would also chase each other in the water and play hide and seek in the reeds and long grasses along the river banks. Also, as the cattle rested, we ourselves would fight. Boys of the same age would engage in fist fights which began playfully but more often than not ended in tears and bruises. As part of our play, we would also make carts with wooden "tyres" and roll them downhill paths

2

to the river. After riding on the cart downhill; one had to carry it uphill. We never got tired of this particular game. Hence it was repeated several times.

In 1954, at the age of nine, my step-brother Kiiru instructed my mother to take me to Mihuti Primary School. Once there, I was received by a famous teacher called Charles. As I registered, I could hear the instruction of an English teacher whom I later learned was called Stephen Maina of Kiairathe Village. He was telling the pupils to lift up heavy stones and repeat after him certain words. I could hear him say, "Boys say after me: 'I am holding a stone,'" and they would repeat 'I am holding a stone.' I picked this one phrase. When we went home after admission and registration we practised the new words we had learned with other standard one recruits to the astonishment of my mother. My mother preferred I do not go to school, but she deferred to my step-brother Kiiru whom she respected immensely.

Jotham Kiiru was born in 1920. He went to Mihuti Primary School between 1936 and 1940. In 1941, he joined the East African Railways and Harbours where he stayed until 1966 when he retired. In 1949 he married a beautiful woman Zipporah Wanjiru. They have lived together ever since. Their first baby was a girl Waiyego born in 1951. Other children who followed are Karuga, Wanjiku, Wairimu, Muthoni, Njoki, Thuita, Charagu, Wamuguru and Mwenda. Kiiru's family is indeed my second family. I have always looked up to Kiiru as my father and we are great friends. He is now a prominent businessman and a farmer.

After registration, I started attending school the following Monday. Never before in my life had I worn a shirt and a pair of shorts. Like other classmates, I had great difficulties in putting on the shorts. Some of my classmates even left their

3

shorts behind in class when they went to answer to a call of nature. Often I used to wear my shorts through one leg. The teachers would laugh until tears welled in their eyes.

Six months after I was registered in school, the Emergency became so severe that our school had to be closed. I was transferred together with other boys to Ngutu Primary School. Ngutu being very far from home and very dangerous to travel to then, I could not continue with my education. I think I went to Ngutu Primary School for only one term.

By this time, I was big enough to understand what the emergency was all about. In early 1952, our house was used as an oathing centre. My mother was among the women who were trusted by the Movement. Our house was also used as a passage centre for oath takers before they were moved to various other oath taking destinations.

I remember one day, as I lay on my mother's bed, I could see people waiting to be transported to another oathing centre trying to remove all the ornaments on their hands and neck. Some who had difficulties in easily removing theirs because they had out-grown them, were beaten badly and forced to remove them. Some had to cut them. There was one woman I loved very much. I saw her being beaten by someone through a chink in the timber wall that separated my mother's bedroom from the fire place. I felt very sorry for her and so I decided to shout at the person beating her. I did not realise, of course, the seriousness of screaming and when I shouted to her to cry out, a guard came right into the bedroom where I was. Almost instantaneously other guards who appeared quite ruthless came and I was measured against a rifle's length. Fortunately I was the same height as the rifle and so I was spared. I was later told that if I had been taller than the rifle, I would have been shot. As a precautionary measure, I was moved to my

4

step-brother's house uphill about one mile from my mother's house. I had to stay in the house alone because my step-brother's wife and children were in Nairobi. I was securely locked inside. I cried until I settled at the main door where I slept. My mother came to my step-brother's house in the morning to enquire about me. She was extremely happy to see me because she was not told where I had been taken. Indeed she thought I had been killed.

In 1954, the emergency reached its climax. I can vividly remember one day before I stopped going to school at Ngutu Primary School. During that day I was coming from school with some other boys. As we approached the famous Thuguri Hill near Mr. Karaba's house, two Mau Mau men then known as terrorists emerged from the forest. They were being chased by homeguards. They ran past us and we could hear not only the shooting but also the sound of bullets. We did not realise the danger we were in until Mzee Karaba ordered us to lie down flat. I think the homeguards realised we were only children and let us alone. The Mau Mau men also passed without bothering much about us. Among them was a man called Muchiri Njogu who later became the Headman of Karunge Village after my family moved there.

Perhaps the greatest Mau Mau battle I ever witnessed was the famous fight at South Mathioya bridge where a District Officer, nicknamed *Kandara* was murdered. It was about four o'clock and my mother was preparing porridge. We heard the sound of different guns about 3 miles in the direction of Kagumo Hill. The sound of the guns was so loud that everything else seemed to stop. I overheard people saying the bullets were falling like rain. After about one hour of battle, we then heard a trumpet. We were told by those who knew what it meant, that it was the Mau Mau's sign of victory. That night people were really scared. My mother and other women knew what would happen the following day and indeed it happened. At about six o'clock in the morning, we were awakened by the smoke of burning houses. The entire Rwathia and all the area between the Godo and Mathioya rivers all the way to the forest was declared by the government a prohibited area and anyone found in that area would be shot at sight. The whole night people from the affected areas came to our place. They filled our ridge with their animals and all that they could carry. Then all houses in the affected areas were burnt and any moving object killed.

During this counter-offensive, I saw a white man for the first time, I believe a K.A.R. soldier standing near river Godo. He was asking the homeguards what they were doing and since we did not know English then, we failed to understand what he was saying. We thought he was making the noise of a person who wants to sneeze but does it so loudly and through the mouth. He kept saying: '*What io wara you doing*'. This became a saying among us boys afterwards.

Death became the order of the day. Many people were killed on the assumption that they were *Mau Maus* Afterwards we were forced to go and view the dead bodies.

I remember one day about four Mau Mau men were killed at Riaita, near a famous bridge called Mburi ya Njuru. This was a grassy area where animals used to drink water. The dead Mau Mau men were piled together and dry banana leaves placed on them. The homeguards then boasted that they had finished all the Mau Mau terrorists. It was then very difficult to sleep after witnessing such a horrible sight. People smelt death everywhere. Our parents as well as other grown-up men and women wept when they saw their brothers lying dead. We could see that they felt death could come any time.

The whole area was filled with the shadow of death. Even as we went to look after cows with other boys, we would find dead bodies in the wattle tree plantations. Often we saw many flies buzzing above the same spot. When we threw stones to make them fly away, we would find it was a human hand or leg that lay there.

However, I will never forget the night when Field Marshal Dedan Kimathi passed through our village on his way to the forest. News came from the men in my place Gathigia that Kimathi was to pass through Gathigia on his way to Nyandarua from an inspection tour of his armies on the other side of the forest.

Lots of goats were collected from individual homes in the locality. My mother's house was very large and so it was selected to be the place where Kimathi would rest while his food was being prepared. When he came into the house he was given a stool. He had three generals with him. He was exceptionally well dressed in a very clean uniform. In fact he looked like a general by present standards. His deputies were equally well dressed. My mother had at her disposal three other women to assist her in preparing the food for this great man of Kenya. Kimathi was served in a very special way. A full goat, that is every piece of meat of full goat was placed in a traditional tray with two knives. He took one knife, turned the pieces on the tray to find out whether there was any missing piece. Finding every piece on the tray, he cut a small piece from one of the limbs and ate it. He then passed the knife to a younger soldier who was called from outside. I later learned that he was his ADC (Aide de Camp). The meat was cut into pieces and they ate. I too was given a big piece. Kimathi was very friendly indeed. He did not stay for long. After he ate, he gave me two shillings and told me that if the war continued, we the young ones, would grow tall enough to join in the fight. I felt very happy at the prospect of joining the fight in the future. I already knew why we were fighting, because I had learned this in the many songs that we sang in praise of Kenyatta and Kimathi.

So after eating and giving me two shillings, women were called in and they made 'ululations of joy' as we say in Kikuyu, *ithano cia kahii*. He was then escorted away. Many girls helped to carry his food to the forest. We thought that they would never come back but the following day, they all came back and they told us horrifying stories about the forest.

As days went by, the fight became very intense. Aeroplanes started bombing the Aberdares. We would go on top of Thunguri hill to witness the bombing from safety.

The homeguards became so cruel that they killed people on mere suspicion. They killed a friend of mine called Kihato. His brother Maruri was my boyhood friend. The night Kihato was killed I could not sleep; it was a terribly frightening night.

Despite all the cruelties of the homeguards and the KAR soldiers, the Mau Mau struggle continued. The government unable to defeat the Mau Mau men finally moved us to new villages. Such a move was aimed at isolating the Mau Mau. We moved to Karunge in 1955. My mother built our house with the assistance of her friends. In fact the whole village was completed in less than six months. When the houses were completed, a fence was put up surrounding the entire village. We helped to transport rafters from where they were obtained to the village. Life was terrible in the village. The pit latrines were open with only logs across the hole. As one helped himself, one could see other peoples faeces with lots of maggots wriggling on them.

Food became scarce. Our parents did communal labour all the time and had only one hour to go to the reserves and to their gardens to collect food. Such food was not enough, we ate only once a day, in the evening. The fare was not food really but some greens with a few maize grains and when one was given his share, it was never enough. To add to these miseries, the houses were full of fleas and bedbugs. We slept on a bare floor together with my mother and covered ourselves with her calico sheet which was the only cloth she had. All night long the bedbugs and fleas would dutifully prey on us. Worse still were the jiggers. They were everywhere in our bodies: in our toes, our fingers, our buttocks and sometimes even the lips. It was madness. God had really deserted his people. I really could not understand.

When we children were left at home, we learned to supplement the little food we got from our mothers. After our parents left for the communal labour, we would go out and hunt for grasshoppers which we would roast in tins. They were a delicacy.

We had also identified a type of edible grass. When schools opened, those boys who went to school also brought back to us beans securely hidden in their shorts' pockets which we fried in tins and ate. Despite our varied assortment of food there were hardly any stomachaches then.

The homeguards were very cowardly. They would fire guns all the night to ostensibly scare the Mau Mau even when there was none. Whenever they were told their camps would be attacked, they would force the whole village to scream all night so as to scare away the Mau Mau. If the occupants of a particular house were found quiet, they would be beaten to death.

We also learnt to dance the *muthiuro*, a game for boys and girls so that we could collect maize from houses in the village. What we used to do was gather a group of boys, give ourselves names and then move to individual houses without making any noise. When we reached the door, we would start the dance with *ibege* tied to our legs. We would be given a maize cob or money. Then we would sing praises to the husband and wife of that house and pray that the couple be blessed with thirty boys and thirty girls. In any house where nothing was given to us or where the owners refused to open the door when they were capable of giving us maize or money, we would curse them and move on to the next house. That way we managed to collect a lot of maize and money. The girls, too, would do the same. I was very good in leading the songs for the big boys and my dance name was *Kamwamba*. After all that was done, we would find one of the houses that was unoccupied and make a feast. This feast would sometimes last for a week. Sometimes we joined the girls and then we would really have fun. Apparently girls started fascinating me a long time ago.

It was while I was at Karunge Village, that I had my first ride on a vehicle. There was a lorry that used to come and collect manure from the village to a homeguard's shamba. He had started planting coffee. We would be given a ride in the lorry and in turn load and unload the manure. This was great fun. I held myself tight on the body-work of the lorry because everything was going round, the trees, bananas, people and so on. When the lorry stopped, we were not able to come out immediately because we felt dizzy. We would look at the driver of the vehicle, a famous Mr. Kanyogo, in awe as he supervised the unloading of the manure. He was however a very nice man. We would do this work the whole day without feeling hungry or tired.

In 1956, my mother moved us to Mihuti Village. She had talked to one man Gakure Minai, an old friend of the family, who agreed to give us one of his houses. We moved into the new house. Mihuti Village was nearer to our shambas. The Emergency had also become less severe and so we could go to our shambas to help our mother.

It was while I was at Mihuti that Kiiru my step-brother sent for me to join him in Nairobi. When the news came to me, I could not believe my ears. I think Kiiru always loved me.

He wanted me to go to Nairobi so that he could make arrangements for me to resume school the following year. I travelled to Gathare Village where I slept in a woman's house. The woman would later escort me to Nairobi. I cannot remember her name, but I think she was a very enlightened woman by the standards of those days. She had very clean children and she was very clean too. I was told her husband worked in Nairobi and that he frequently sent her lots of clothes. The night I spent in her house was the best in my life up to that time because for the first time, I ate chapatis to my full satisfaction. I could not believe that it was possible to eat chapati until one was fully satisfied and could not eat any more. Chapati to me at that time was so special, that it was only meant for a special class of people. Never before had I eaten these special items to my satisfaction. It was really great indeed. I wished and prayed that I could only be allowed to look after the children of this woman so that I could always eat well.

The day I was to travel to Nairobi started very well. An old man called Njema who had a lorry came to the house and had breakfast with us. We then proceeded to the lorry which was parked up the hill near Gathare School. I was informed that I would travel at the back of the lorry while the woman stayed in front. There was a lot of luggage at the back of the lorry, but I did not mind at all. There were also two turnboys with me. As we travelled to Nairobi, we passed through Gikoe, Nyakianga, Ngutu, Gitugi and for the first time I saw Mathioya Dam before we arrived at Murang'a. The dam was so large that I had to close my eyes to stop seeing it. To make it worse, the lorry travelled along the edge and it became a horrible sight. However, we moved uphill and left the dam behind.

Eventually, we arrived in Murang'a Town. I could not believe my eyes when I saw the many shops in the town. They were so many that I could not count them. I also saw the tarmac road. This too, I could not believe. How can a road be so black and free from dust? We stopped at Murang'a where the driver and his turnboys had some food. I was given half a loaf of bread to eat all by myself. I could not believe it. I said to myself, 'These people must be very generous. How could they give me all that bread alone? If it were back in the village, I would have to share the bread with many boys, may be ten. Everyone would eat a very small piece indeed'. I remembered my friends in the village and my mother and wished it were possible to have her share the bread with me. However, I finished eating it all and we started off for Nairobi.

From Murang'a Town, we travelled on the tarmac all the time. As we were about to cross Maragua River, I saw a very huge bridge on the river and I inquired from the turnboys what it was. I was told it was the railway bridge over the Maragua River. Of course, it was a strange sight to me then. I had a very good view of it from the top of the lorry. Soon thereafter we crossed the Maragua River itself. The river was no doubt bigger than our famous Godo River from where I

12

used to drink water every day. We moved on and for the first time, I saw a railway crossing and railway lines. I asked the turnboy friends whether we would see any train. They replied I would see many trains in Nairobi.

We moved fast to Thika. We travelled right into the town centre, parked our lorry at the bus stage and the driver gave some time to take a break and pass water. I went to a Council toilet and helped myself. I saw the Kenya Bus Service bus from Nairobi, and also double-decker buses. Once back at the top of the lorry, I could see the passengers on the upper decker but could not understand how they had climbed up there. We then moved out of the town towards Nairobi. Since the town looked too big for me, I could not recognise where we came in and where we went out through. In fact I had thought Thika was Nairobi. We proceeded to Nairobi arriving via Kariokor Market. There I was handed over to Mrs. Wambui Kimemia who was to take me to Makongeni Estate where Kiiru and his family lived. By this time, I was muddled up. I could not know for sure where I was nor could I say which direction was East, West, North or South. If Wambui had left me at Kariokor Market I would have got lost. I could see people making different kinds of *mandazi* from the ones I knew of back in the village which were only a ten cent each and very small. The Kariokor *mandazi* were so big that one needed only one for a meal. I wished Mrs. Kimemia would buy me one. Luck was indeed with me though. One person identified me as the son of Njeri. He proceeded to ask me what I wanted to have. I replied I wanted a *mandazi*. The kind man bought for me a *mandazi* and some *chai*. I quickly devoured the snack. It was delicious and I enjoyed it. Whenever I pass through Kariokor even today, I remember the *mandazi* and *chai*.

We did not stay for long at Kariokor. We took a bus to Makongeni. As we moved, I could not help wondering how human beings made such tall buildings that almost touched the sky. The buildings were so tall that I could not help pitying the person who lived at the top. I suspected such persons could fall easily from such a dizzying height.

We moved fast and soon reached Makongeni. We alighted and proceeded to my step-brother's house. There I found that they lived in a one-roomed house. The children had their cot while the parents' bed was next to the cot. I had to sleep on the floor. I did not blame my step-brother and his wife because they had really tried. I thought Wanjiru, my step-brother's wife must be a very kind woman because other wives would not have allowed me to come to Nairobi when they had an accommodation problem. To this day I am always grateful for this sacrifice made by her.

Soon, I made friends with many boys and I learnt many city games. I learnt some little Kiswahili and could sometimes move through the estate at night. I also learnt how to ride a bicycle. Mr. Muragi Iya, whose son Maina became a great friend of mine, allowed me to ride his bicycle. When I became an expert, I would ride to Bahati from Makongeni.

Evening classes were organised for me at Bahati Primary School. I did very well in those classes. However, it was very dangerous to move to Bahati at night, because first I had to cross Jogoo Road then known as Donholm Road. I had then to proceed along Bahati Road on which the KBS buses were driven very recklessly. I remember one day as I proceeded to school along a very narrow pathway on one side, there was the road and on the other, a fence of barbed wires. As I was walking, a double-decker KBS bus approached me. I was convinced it was going to fall on me. It was being driven so carelessly that it almost ran over me. So to avoid it, I leaned towards the fence and my ears were badly injured by the barbed wire. I went to school feeling a lot of pain. Seeing my sorry state, the teacher sent me home. However, I did not want to go home alone, so I waited outside for the other boys. When I went home, Wanjiru was very sympathetic, though there was no medicine at home. The wounds healed by and by.

Times were also very hard in Nairobi. I used to escort Wanjiru to Buru Buru to dig a small shamba that she owned. In the meantime, I would look after Waiyego, Karuga and Wanjiku. Sometimes I would also dig. Wanjiru's shamba is now part of the present Buru Buru Estate.

As the year closed, Kiiru directed that I should go to Standard One in Mihuti at the beginning of 1957. Wanjiru was ordered to go with me to the village. At the beginning of the year, she took me to Mihuti Primary School, where I again re-registered in Standard One. I was a big boy then aged twelve. I had even learnt how to seek out girls of my age.

Chapter Two

SCHOOL DAYS

School life at Mihuti was very exciting. We started learning immediately under a famous teacher for Standard One called Abiud. Since I was already a big boy, I did well. I was number two in the first term behind a boy called Gaituri who was older than me. I was not yet baptised, so I started the Bible classes and I was baptised while I was still at Mihuti Primary School. Baptismal classes were difficult then because you had to go through several stages. You had to be a 'Muthikiriria' then 'Mucharia', finally a 'Muthomagi' and then you were baptised. I was baptised in an old mud church house by Revered Felix Nyoro of Gathukiru. My godfather was the late Francis Muchoba who suggested that I should be baptised Samuel, although I had wanted to be called Robert. Since I was like Samuel of the Bible as I was the only son of my mother, I could not argue and so I was baptised Samuel. I made a very small feast to celebrate this occasion because I had no money. It was very hard to raise the school fees those days which was Shs. 20/- for the whole year plus Shs. 3/- for cess. Kiiru would contribute Shs. 20/- and tell my mother to look for the balance of Shs. 3/-. It took her several nights to borrow the money from her women friends. However, she had always managed things and somehow she managed even then.

There were lots of interesting things in the school. I was always overjoyed on Friday afternoons when we had singing lessons. We could learn new Christian songs, write them in our music books and sing them the whole afternoon. We had a very good time because the music teacher would sometimes leave us singing and go away.

During this time, I also became very interested in story telling. On Thursday afternoons, we would be asked to volunteer to tell stories. I remember the teacher would often tell me to put down my hand because I wanted to tell many stories. My mother would tell me the stories at night preceding the day of story telling and I would in turn tell them to the class. It was very difficult for some boys to speak in front of the class but somehow I managed.

We also enjoyed going to the field to collect leaves for compost manure. When we went with the girls, we would arrange that the boys collect sufficient leaves for them so that later we would have fun.

Then the final year in primary school came. This was 1960 when I was in Standard 4. We had to sit the Common Entrance Examination, in short CEE. One had to pass it before proceeding to intermediate school. It was thus a very important examination done in the second term. I was advised by my mother that the best way to pass the examination was to eat a 'luck sweet potato' on the morning of the examination. It was a special sweet potato from a famous sweet potato vein called *kando*. I ate it before eating anything else that morning. I did so and then went to sit for the examination at Rwathia Primary School about four miles from our village. On that day, it was very cold, but we did not have any pullovers or coats.

After the examination, we stayed the entire third term before the results were known. Before we closed for the December holiday, they were announced. I had passed and was admitted to Rwathia Intermediate School. I think I passed because I had prepared myself adequately but at that time, I believed like my mother that it was the 'Luck Sweet Potato' that enabled me to pass. My other friends were admitted to other neighbouring Intermediate Schools such as Thuguri, Njumbi and Kangema in Murang'a.

At Rwathia, I started well. The fees had now been raised to Shs. 60/- per year. We walked every morning the four miles with other boys from Mihuti village to school. Bethwel Macharia, Mureithi Ndegwa, Gakanya Maina were all from Mihuti Village. We had to wake up very early indeed because we had to collect all the other things required for school, these being rafters, ashes, cow dung and water. We had to carry several kilos of cow dung to school. Besides all that, we had to be punctual for school.

In that school I did very well and I became number 9 in the first term in Standard 5, then number 2 in the second term, then number 1 for the following terms until I finished the Intermediate School in 1963. I did Kenya Preliminary Examination in 1963 in Standard 7 together with Standard 8 pupils. Fortunately, I passed very well with 'A's in all subjects.

Just before I went to Secondary School, a major event took place in our country. We were granted independence by the British on 12th December, 1963. As Jomo Kenyatta would want us to say, 'We snatched' our independence from the British. It was a day of great celebrations. We sang at night and moved from Mihuti to Rwathia singing songs of praise to our great leader Jomo Kenyatta. There was a lot of rain and we all got wet but we did not care at all. We walked in the rain amid lots of fun and happiness. It was the end of colonial rule from which we had suffered too much during the emergency.

I had chosen Nyeri Boys for my High School. My

admission to Nyeri Boys was very much delayed. Most boys were called earlier than myself. My friend Joseph Gakanya Maina and I were almost the two sure cases that were not called initially. We felt very worried but each one of us prayed to God in his own way and sure enough we received our letters of admission. Maina was called to Njiri's High School while I was admitted to Ichagaki Secondary School. Before this year I had only known Maina as one of the village boys and as a member of our famous 'G.I.C.U.' organisation that is, the Gorumatical Indestructable Correspondence Union. This was a body which we had started to enable us to prepare for the examination. Other members of the Union included Jimna Gakuo, Muikamba and Bernard Thuku. It was indeed very useful because all the members did well in the Kenya Preliminary Examination which it assisted us to prepare for. The name Gorumatical is not English. It was derived from the name of an imaginary animal, a Colossus that we believed lived under the *Mururi* tree along the Godo River on what is now Maina Gakuo's shamba. We all feared the animal and our naming the organisation after it was to show our respect and fear to the mighty animal.

Joseph Gakanya Maina was just a member of the G.I.C.U. organisation and little did I know that he would later become my closest friend. I became his best man in his wedding and he too was my best man. With the passage of time we have become friends all the more.

Both of us gained admission to Secondary School. I proceeded to Ichagaki Secondary School. During early January, I found Ichagaki to be a very difficult school because in the first place, it was a day school. Hence we had to provide for our own accommodation and food. I was lucky because I met one boy by the name Stephen Kiiru, a son of

Kiiru's sister-in-law who helped me adjust to the difficult situation.

However, Stephen did not save me from harassment by other old boys. It was customary in most of the secondary schools that the newcomers popularly known as 'Njukas' were mistreated and mishandled. Ichagaki was no exception. We were made to walk bare foot on stones. We were also forced to eat raw bananas and were kicked around by practically all senior students. We were even ordered to wash their clothes.

To make matters worse, the older boys took us to hidden places where we were stripped naked. This was to find out who was circumcised and who was not. Those who had lied that they were circumcised while they were not were badly beaten. I decided that after we closed the school I would have to be circumcised to lessen the harassment. Later after settling in the school, I wrote an article for the school magazine regarding the harassment of form ones. When going through my high school days' papers, I discovered the article itself from the school magazine, *Ichagaki Index.*

WHY BEAT FORM ONES?

It has grown to be a habit in almost every secondary school to beat up form ones as they appear for their first term in the school. This does not only affect the form ones' morale, but also has created a very bad picture of African Students.

What did you feel yourself when on your first day in school you received so much beating instead of much warm welcome? Did you feel yourself inside a civilized or barbaric society? It is true that when form ones come they are beaten thoroughly. Some of them are even kept awake in the dormitories, some are punished heavily, forced to clean latrines or even given bad and unreasonable work which, of course does not benefit anyone. Now to all students I ask, 'Why beat form ones?'

Why punish your brothers, your fellow countrymen and friends? All those of you who are Kikuyus know that when a bull is put into a bull-shed, occupied by many others, it is fought dangerously by them and sometimes it may be killed. But friends, do we want to turn schools into bull-sheds occupied by bulls who must fight any other bull that comes in?

From my own point of view, a school is an institution where we expect to find civilized students quite different from bulls. My fellow students, if you are found by a foreign headmaster beating form ones and he calls you bulls or other barbaric savage names, would you be annoyed? I suppose not since you are performing bulls' actions.

Let us not spoil our good name by performing barbaric, savage and uncivilized actions of beating up our brothers, but instead try to act with a sense of civilization. Let us welcome our form ones, teach them about our school, introduce them to ourselves, please them and they will really feel that they have entered paradise. They will feel themselves living in a civilized and highly understanding society, a place where good manners and good treatment have rooted themselves and where the human soul is highly honoured. Let us not believe that the way to teach form ones discipline is to beat them but instead realise that beating and happiness do not live in one house.

SAMUEL KARUGA WANDAI

21

From the time I was baptised in 1960 at Mihuti Anglican Church, I tried my best to be a good Christian. When I went to Ichagaki Secondary School, which was a Catholic school, it became very hard for me to participate in religious activities. We were not given choice of denominations. We all had to go to the Catholic Church every morning and every evening irrespective of what denomination one belonged to. Most of us therefore embraced Catholicism. I was rebaptised Reginald Karuga Wandai. During the baptism, a friend of mine, Simon Mwangi, became my god-father. From then I became a Catholic and I am still one today, and so too is my entire family. My mother later followed suit and was rebaptised Lucy.

When we closed for April vacation and I decided to be circumcised, I asked John Zakaria, an old friend of mine, to take me to Kangema where I was circumcised. From then on, I acquired a licence to speak to the big girls. When we re-opened school I announced I was a man not a boy, a *mundurume* not a *kihii*. I had graduated to another stage in life.

It was not my intention to join student's politics in Ichagaki, but I found myself in it. I became an active member of the school debating society. We had debates usually on Fridays. We had many motions. I remember one time when we were debating a motion 'Whether or not it was necessary to be circumcised', I supported the motion that circumcision was necessary for boys. On my way out, I met the Headmaster at the door waiting for me. Apparently he had been listening to the debate. He asked me whether circumcision was as important as I had argued.

I answered it was, because only after circumcision would one be permitted to speak with big girls. I informed him that as a Reverend he did not know the importance of a girl. He was very amused. I thought I was going to be punished, but to my surprise this did not happen.

At Mihuti Village we also engaged in student politics. A group of students started an organisation called 'Thanguri Educated Fellows Association', TEFA in short. I was elected as its first president while other officials included Isaiah Ngotho Kariuki and my friend Joseph Gakanya Maina.

It also included students in High School from the two neighbouring villages namely Karunge and Ngutu. I travelled to these villages making speeches and explaining the provisions of our constitution. The association was very successful. Indeed we hosted several parties.

In the school, I was elected Chairman of the Hostel Committee. The hostel had been completed, but the Headmaster, fearing problems from the boarders, did not want to involve himself in the running of the hostel. So he left the responsibility to us. Other officers elected with me were Paul Kamau, popularly known as Nkrumah or Adam Smith for his knowledge of economics, George Kaniu now with the Ministry of Commerce and Industry and another gentleman from Kiaira, a village in Kangema, called Kamau Titus. We had to take care of everything including discipline in the hostel and also the buying of supplies. I collected Shs. 4,000/- from the boarding students every beginning of term to run the hostel for the whole term. One time, I dreamt about someone coming to steal this money which I had kept in my box waiting for the morning so that I could take it to the headmaster for safe keeping. I screamed and the whole hostel woke up. Karanja, who used to sleep on the lower decker bed, jumped to my upper bed to escape from whoever had come. I called him, *'nyoka'* (snake) and we held each other very tightly thinking he was the thief. The hostel was later quietened. Up to today, Karanja and myself call each other 'Nyoka' whenever we meet.

One incident that happened at Ichagaki during those days will never be forgotten. The boys of Kanyai Village were very jealous of us because they thought we were taking their girls from them due to our education. They complained that their girls liked us more than them. So they decided to lay an ambush and attack us on our way to the hostel from night studies. Because the hostel was outside the school compound, we had to travel outside the compound to our sleeping places. It was late in the evening at about 11.30 p.m. when the generator was put off. We moved in a group out of the gate and on reaching an unusually dark corner we were attacked indiscriminately by the local boys and beaten badly with sticks and clubs. Fortunately, they did not have *pangas* or *simis*.

We were scattered by our attackers with some of us running to a nearby plantation. We lost direction completely and some of us slept in the banana shamba until the following morning. This of course worked well for the Kanyai boys because from then on we stopped going to the village to look for girls. At least not as often as before, and therefore they enjoyed their girls alone.

Everyone who passed through Ichagaki Secondary School has memories of Father Vidoli. He was an Italian who really hated Africans. Because of this he never called us by name. We were all referred to by numbers like prisoners. I was number 27 in our class. One time I had a dangerous confrontation with him because of some political differences. I was not happy about his hatred for Africans and particularly after our hard won Uhuru. So I argued with him on political matters in class. He called me a communist and ordered me out of the classroom. I resisted but he insisted that either I had to go out or he would go out himself. I did not go out so he went and called the headmaster, Reverend Father Deleide also an Italian priest whom I think never liked Father Vidoli. He reported me to the headmaster who was on the school verandah. The headmaster listened to him patiently and then he requested me to go back to class. Father Vidoli was very upset and so he told Father Deleide the headmaster that, "If he goes back to class, then you will teach them English", but Father Deleide simply ignored him.

I did not do well in my examination because of being involved in too many activities within the school and outside. Moreover, I was often out of class because of lack of school fees. Due to the same problem, I wanted to drop out at Form II and join a Teachers College as a P2, but somehow I managed to raise enough money for Form III and IV. At this time my step-brother who was educating me had his children also in school and with his small salary at the Railways, it was not very easy to manage.

However, despite all the difficulties, I managed to pass with division II of 25 points. I wanted to do two things. I had chosen law and also teaching. I wanted a job where I would use my mouth and my mind.

During my Form III and Form IV, I read a lot on economics and politics in our school library. I also wrote many essays on political and other subjects. As I went through my papers written at Ichagaki Secondary School, I found the following essays which I think are of some interest. I reproduce the first one in its original form.

25

Democracy, Democracy is the common cry for every Kenyan, but what type of Democracy? Is one party state a real Democracy or a direct abuse to it?

The KPU founders have realised that one party democracy is the first stage towards dictatorship and tyranny—it is the greatest threat to Lincoln's Democracy, 'Government of the people by the people ....' I am sure everyone in Kenya, who has advocated the injustices imposed on us by KANU Government cannot fail to hail the operation. The opposition is trying to fight against these injustices. You all have witnessed how the President has detained people without any legal trial. Is this not the exact tyranny? The opposition is using all its efforts to fight against these inhuman activities by the so called KANU Government. How many unemployed and landless persons do we have in Kenya and what is the government doing about this? Only the Ministers are still adding to themselves fat pay and bigger land. Your glorious opposition is totally opposed to these notable corruptions.

Can we change this KANU Government by the use of our military? Yes, this is the only way if there is no opposition. Therefore the Kenya People's Union, the only party that is interested in the poor man, is ready to form an alternative government if commissioned by its people to do so. Everyone knows the basic policies of our KPU is land for the landless, employment for the unemployed, and above all, free education and health facilities for our poor citizens. Long live our dear party.

Would you like to laugh a little bit? Then I advise you to open the KPU manifesto. The first policy is Free things for everyone. But who can provide free things for everyone? Will the so called Kenya People's Union create economic goods to raise Kenya's wealth to a level where everything would be free?

Look at the United States, the richest country in the world. How many people there get free things? Hail, Kuwait the country with the largest income per capita. How many people get everything free there? Then, why listen or waste time with such a destructive and aimless party which advocates such foolish policies? Our citizens are honourable, intelligent and morally conscious not to be cheated by a group of hungry individuals who are seeking for power.

Are they really hungry for power or can they provide a genuine leadership? Check the leadership behind KPU. The personalities who failed to win public support when they were in KANU, the people who failed to co-operate with their fellow colleagues, today say that they can form an alternative government better than that of Mzee Kenyatta. Oh yes, an alternative government, communist government for who? For us Kenyans? Think, dear citizen, what KPU is after.

If KPU's claim is to rescue the national economy, why is it following a tribalistic pattern—Oginga or rather double Os or Rs as you like, Okello Odongo or rather Ochieng Oneko the KPU boss, all Luos? What more evidence do you need dear citizens? Reject communism, or to quote its own words 'Scientific Socialism'.

Another essay which I wrote in Secondary School concerned my vision of a beautiful wife. It was entitled "My Beautiful Wife," and read as follows:

It was in the afternoon. The 2 p.m. bell had gone. I went into the classroom and prepared for a Mathematics lesson which was on Geometry.

'Afternoon boys', the teacher said. We all stood up and answered his greetings. 'Take out your geometry books', he ordered. He started drawing a figure on the blackboard. All I saw was that it was a semi-circle. Then slowly I drifted from the lesson, and soon was far away in England.

I had passed my High School Cambridge Examinations and I was now admitted into the London School of Economics for a degree in political science. I was very lucky because in my class there were some really beautiful girls. They did not like me until at the end of my course.

It was during the graduation ceremony that one girl Catherine by name was seated beside me. 'Samuel', she called, 'You are going back to Kenya after this'? I looked at her and she smiled. 'Oh yes, next week', I answered. 'Next week!' she exclaimed. 'We shall talk over that matter after this,' she said.

After the ceremony there was a great reception made in our honour. Catherine sat by my side every moment and kept on talking to me. Surely, she loved me but I had not realized. After the reception we parted but she promised to come and see me before I left for Kenya. When she came, I was ready to welcome her. We had one day's stay together and indeed, it was so lovely that I will never forget it. She persuaded me to stay for another week with her and even promised to meet all my expenses during the stay. She took me to her parents and introduced me to them. Her father was a politician and her mother a social worker. 'Samuel, I love you' she whispered holding me tight. She had stolen my speech, my motion and my power of reasoning. What could I do? 'Do you really mean it Catherine?' I asked. She told the parents that she loved me and they were happy about it. I wrote home and I was allowed to marry.

In the University, Catherine, now my wife, had graduated in sociology, so she was of utmost importance in my public life. When I arrived in Kenya, I found a job for her with the Social Services in Kenya. I got a job with the KANU political party where I was fully engaged in politics. Each of us did very well as we were both London graduates. Every night we were together, discussing and preparing my political speeches, and at the same time picking up most of the day's criticisms against my party.

'You do these problems during prep and we shall go over them tomorrow', the Mathematics master said leaving the classroom. Am I in class? Am I not with my beautiful Catherine? Where is she? In Nairobi? Oh! my Catherine.

At last I realized that it was nothing but a day dream that had brought Catherine so near to me.

HOW FAR PEOPLE SHOULD BE FREE TO SPEAK AND WRITE AS THEY WISH IN KENYA

People of Kenya should be allowed as much freedom to speak and write as possible so long as the people concerned do not use this freedom to destroy the good name of Kenya.

Artists should be free to practise any art, but they should be restricted not to draw pictures which will not be valuable to the country. Any of the artists who tries to draw pictures of people who are primitive as an example of modern Kenya should be warned to stop this sort of art because it would spoil the good name of our country. But, any artist who aims at developing his art on the basis of promoting Kenya's good name should be encouraged for the good of our country.

Most of the writers tend to write only books useful for educational purposes. Such people should be encouraged to carry on this valuable work because it benefits the nation, but if a writer devotes himself to writing books on ideologies that will stir up the minds of the millions, and thus encourage riots within the country, he should be strictly prohibited. If a man dedicates himself to writing novels, stories and some interesting prose, he should be encouraged because the nation needs many stories for recreation. All writers should bear in mind that they should only write books which will benefit the nation.

Not only can writing bring good or bad to the Kenyan nation, but also the country's politicians. Most of the politicians are good people who want to see a stable government flourishing in Kenya by speaking and writing on the good things of the country. A good politician should not interfere with the stability of the country by writing and speaking of impossible things. It is clear that every politician has some followers, and they will accept all that he says or writes because they believe in his political activities. If politicians are not careful, they can create instability in Kenya which would be harmful to our country's prosperity. But suppose all the politicians speak only what is good for our country, suppose they find it useless to be ambitious, if they only think in terms of national unity, then Kenya would safely prosper. In other words, politicians should speak out realism, write and practise the National Unionism.

A private citizen can bring good or bad to the country and therefore it should be realised that he devotes his whole love either to the good of Kenya or to the harm of it. So if he is of the latter quality he will write everything that happens in Kenya under the term 'bad'. So, he will not mind how much the name of Kenya is spoiled. If such a man is given this freedom, he will spoil the nation and so he should be deprived of it as soon as he is found abusing it.

Since in all democratic countries, the press is said to govern public opinion, then the press and all public publications should be restricted so that they will produce only what is good for Kenya. They should not be allowed to print things that will mislead our people.

All speaking, writing, publishing, or drawing should be made only to add taste to the good name of Kenya and its people.

Chapter Three

LAW SCHOOL

After completion of my 'O' level education, I moved to Nairobi to look for a job. None of us school leavers knew whether we would be employed or even pass the examination itself. I was given accommodation by Samuel Maina Mwangi, a relative of mine at Makongeni. He had one room which we both shared.

During the day, I joined other school leavers in search of a job. We went to many offices in Nairobi, and everywhere we went we were confronted by the notice "no vacancy". It was not unusual for one to go the whole day without food. Sometimes I would go to Gikomba to my brother-in-law's place. My brother-in-law, Mr. Shadrack Gichuhi Githinji, used to sell second hand clothes. He would give me two shillings which I would then use to buy food from the kiosks at thirty cents per plate. Two shillings would stretch for a long time. All school leavers in Nairobi would congregate on Tom Mboya Street where all our forms for employment were. We took days there and we really got very tired and hungry.

Finally, I was called to the Kenya School of Law for an interview. There were very many other applicants.

After the interview, I got my letter of admission. I could not believe it; it was like a dream come true. I went to St. Peter Claver's Church on Racecourse Road to thank God.

The letter of admission read as follows:

Reference: Gen./40/W.56

Mr. Samuel Karuga Wandai
c/o Jotham Kiiru
P.O. Box 13056
NAIROBI.

Dear Sir,

APPLICATION FOR ENTRY TO THE SCHOOL—
APRIL 1968 ENTRY.

With reference to your application for entry to the school, I am very pleased indeed to inform you that you are being offered a place subject to satisfactory reference and a medical examination.

Because the number of entries is limited, I am now writing to all successful candidates to obtain their confirmation that they intend to take up the place offered accordingly. I should be grateful if you will write and confirm that you intend to take up the place offered to you.

Please reply as soon as possible and in any event so as to reach me not later than the 11th of April. A stamped addressed envelope is enclosed so as to enable you to reply.

If I do not hear from you by the 11th of April, I will assume that you do not intend to come to the school. Accordingly your place would be offered to a candidate on the reserve list.

Next term begins on Monday the 29th April, at 8 a.m. New entrants are required to be in residence by noon on Sunday the 28th of April.

We are looking forward to welcoming you at the school and I hope that our association together will be a rewarding one.

Yours very truly,

R.H. MUNRO
PRINCIPAL.

I reported to the school of law in April 1968. At once I decided it was an excellent institution. It was situated in Milimani area which during the colonial times was for Europeans. I was shown to room No. 17 where I was to stay with Matthew Kunyuru. The school had wonderful lecture theatres and a beautiful well stocked library. We found the old boys already well settled. In the school, people were treated well and with a lot of respect. We were addressed by the Principal the late Mr. Munro, who reminded us that we had joined the most honourable profession of law. We were told that we always had to behave properly as befitting members of the honourable profession.

What was amazing in the law school was the food. For the first time, I learned how to use a fork, spoon and knife all at the same time. Moreover, the food at the law school was taken in courses. There was course one, two and three. In the beginning, most of us could not handle the situation. We ate so much bread in the first course that when the main course came, we had already eaten enough. We were really overfed.

Secondly, we never made our beds in the law school. They were made for us and laundry done by attendants. The rooms were well cleaned, all we did was to eat and study. By the previous standards that I was used to, this was really a heaven on earth.

On top of all these nice things we were given some pocket money. We received Shs. 48/- per month and an annual clothing allowance of Shs. 200/-. I bought my first suit then at a price Shs 150/-. It was a very smart suit and when I put it on, I could not believe it was me. When I added a tie, I became even more gorgeous. I could not believe it. This was a place of extreme luxury where students used suits for their uniforms. This was going to be my home for the next five years. I felt great indeed.

One day as I was going to visit my sister Wairimu, I bought them three pounds of meat and when I told them it was from my money, they too could not believe it. That day, we all feasted well. I thought these first days in the Kenya School of Law were very happy indeed. We learnt many other things like going to night clubs. We used to have concessions at Starlight night club where we normally spent most of the weekends after receiving our pocket money. Some students unfortunately finished all the money there. We learnt all kinds of funny things. There were many prostitutes at Starlight and they only asked for a pound (Shs. 20/-). We would then smuggle them to our rooms in the Law School. They really were beasts. They kept one awake the whole night, woke up very early in the morning and left for town. Once she got out of the room, no one would say which particular room she had come from. After she had left, one slept the whole day because of the tiring job done the previous night. Luckily, there was no AIDS those days.

The law school was also very famous for its dinner night which was the most interesting and most awaited-for occasion in the school. Once a month an important guest, I mean a really important guest — the Attorney General, Chief Justice or a Minister, would be invited to come and dine with us. We would prepare ourselves well for this occasion with our black suits and our academic gowns. We were expected to be seated before the guest came in and when the guest did come in, we would then stand up in his honour. We would then be served. There was the high table where the Chief Guest, the Principal, the President of the Students' Union and other important guests would sit. They would be served first after which we were also served. During the dinner, we would all be served with wine. Surely, this was great. After dinner we would be addressed by the guest. Some of the guests read prepared speeches while others spoke spontaneously. We really enjoyed ourselves. I still retain one of the speeches made by Honourable Charles Njonjo, the Attorney General of the day, a very powerful man then. He was popularly known as "Sir Charles Njonjo The Duke of Kabeteshire" because of his notable English manners. The speech I have retained reads as follows:

A SPEECH TO THE KENYA SCHOOL OF LAW STUDENTS BY THE ATTORNEY GENERAL

LEGAL EDUCATION IN KENYA: SOME REFLECTIONS ON THE PAST AND A LOOK INTO THE FUTURE

Having been wined and dined, I now have to sing my supper. But, before coming to the more solemn part of the evening let me relate to you a case which appeals to me, not only because I possess a sense of humour, but I also happen to be the President of the Automobile Association of East Africa. John Squire, aged 36, explained that appearance can be deceptive when he appeared in court on a charge of driving whilst under the influence of drink. Squire said his car veered across a main road centre line because it had defective steering. His unsteady walk was caused by a dislocated bone in his hip and his short finger nails explained the delay in taking his licence out of his wallet, he said. Working underground produced his bloodshed eyes, and arthritis stopped his doing a finger-to-nose test properly. Then Squire pointed out that he fell asleep during police questioning because he was tired after working all day. The verdict not surprisingly after all that—not guilty.

I wonder whether you students of the law of contract have been told of the case in the House of Lords in which that great English Lawyer, F.E. Smith, appeared for the plaintiff. The case concerned a wagering contract in which Smith reminded their Lordships that all such contracts were null and void. In this case, explained Smith, it involved the game of roulette, which as Smith further explained was played with cards. Following this explanation of how roulette was played, the Lord Chancellor delivered the most devastating monosyllable ever heard in a court of law. If you are still not sure what the Lord Chancellor said then you must consult the law reports or R.E. Megarry's "Miscellany at Law"

Something a little less subtle this time: divorce proceedings.

As many of you already know, the petitioner is asked by her advocate before the trial whether he (or she) has a discretion statement to make. Any act of adultery committed by the petitioner must be admitted and included in such a statement. In one such interview the petitioner said to her advocate, "Oh does it count then in the day time?"

Tonight I address a generation of law students who are today reaping the benefits of the harvest which was sown back in 1963, before Uhuru. This, at a time when I suspect that many of you were treading with trepidation the first steps of a Secondary Education with little thought as to what the future held for you, or as to where your education would lead you. These are indeed exciting days. It is not necessary for me to dwell upon the progress which Kenya has made in so many different spheres since independence. I would like to devote myself this evening to legal education in Kenya. Before looking into the future I would like first of all to reflect nostalgically upon the past.

The paths of the law student today are relatively smooth, but I come from a generation of African lawyers who trod a more rocky path, one strewn with all manner of obstacles which had to be overcome but the goal was reached. I think of the late Chiedo More Gem Argwings Kodhek, the Chief Justice, Kitili Mwendwa, the President of Law Society, Sam Waruhiu, the Chairman of B.A.T. Bethwell Gecaga. One is of blessed memory, but these are the pioneers of the African members of the legal profession. None of them read for law with the support of the then Colonial Government. They all ploughed a lonely furrow and managed as best as they could financially. An African was not encouraged to obtain the vitally longed for legal qualifications.

Argwings Kodhek was called to the Bar in 1951. Bethwell Gecaga was called to the Bar in 1956. In fact, Gecaga and I were one time colleagues in my chambers in 1957. He was later to find his fortune in commerce. He was followed by Sam Waruhiu in 1958 and Kitili Mwendwa in 1961. They were the first of the few.

What is obvious about what I have just said is that for many years students wishing to become laywers could not pursue their studies in East Africa. The facilities for legal education in East Africa were dominated and controlled by lawyers mainly trained and qualified in the United Kingdom and India. The lawyers in the public service were also British members of the Colonial Legal Service. All this had to change and the first steps in achieving this were taken in 1963.

In 1963, the Kenya School of Law was established. At first it did not even occupy these premises, but some temporary vacant government offices. The present premises were purchased later in 1964. They were formerly a private Nursing House and converted into a residential institution. Some of you may even wonder to what use your present room was put to. Well, the lounge in Mr. Jackson's flat was formerly an operating theatre. I am glad to say that little blood is spilt in there nowadays. Mr. Jackson's kitchen was formerly the anaesthetist's room although I understand he now keeps there anaesthetics of a different kind. As for the former mortuary premises, it remains empty, although I understand the Principal has given some thought to it being used for student purposes when he has been faced with accommodation problems.

For myself, I am not sure in what form he intended some of you to enter these premises.

Enough with frivolity. Let me return to my main theme. The Kenya School of Law, having been established, began to prepare students for the qualifying examinations of the Council of Legal Education. The School's students as they do today received their practical legal education in the chambers. The theoretical training was received at the school.

Although the first Kenyan Law graduates of the now University of Dar-es-Salaam graduated in 1964, we had to wait until 1968 before the first student of the Kenya School of Law was admitted as an Advocate to the High Court of Kenya. That was John Gachui Mwangi, who has been in private practice with Kaplan and Stratton ever since. Altogether 10 students were admitted in 1968. They were followed by 17 more in 1969 and 19 more in 1970. This year it is estimated that 22 more students will be admitted in 1972 and 23 more students in 1973. At that point one chapter on legal education in Kenya will be closed, but another chapter will open before us. In April 1973, the Kenya School of Law will take on the new mantle of being a postgraduate practical training school.

The changes which have taken place in the structure of legal education in Kenya are now known to you all. Our thoughts on legal education in Kenya have never remained static, they have been kept under constant review. There is no such thing as an ideal system of legal education.

It was decided in 1969 that a Faculty of Law was to be established at the then University College of Nairobi. It was even then decided that the new Faculty be opened on the 1st July, 1970 and in fact I had the privilege of declaring open the new Faculty of Law. But this was only a beginning. The Faculty is now responsible for the academic education of lawyers for professional practice, commerce and industry, central government and local government services and the East African Community. For the training of those seeking to enter the legal profession as Advocates of the High Court of Kenya, the Faculty will co-operate with the Kenya School of Law.

For the moment, the Kenya School of Law is completing the legal education of those students who entered the school up to and including 1968. There are, of course, some University students present tonight who started their legal education at the school in 1969, but who were transferred to the Faculty of Law under the transitional arrangements. You have formed the nucleus of the first and second LLB groups.

As the University students are aware, the degree course is for a period of three academic years. I expect that most of you will be interested in pursuing a career at the Bar. In that case, on graduation the graduate will have to serve a twelve months pupillage in the chambers of a practising advocate of at least five years standing. There is no escape from this period of pupillage. On completion of this, the graduate will then pursue a post-graduate training course at the Kenya School of Law for a period in the region of nine months. It is expected that the first of such graduates will come to the school in April 1973. You will now, no doubt, be speculating on the answers to two questions. What form will the training take and will you be required to take any further examinations of the Council of Legal Education? As for the training programme, the Council of Legal Education, as the body which exercises general supervision and control over legal education in Kenya and which advises the Government in relation thereto, has appointed a working committee consisting of a Council member, Mr. S.N. Waruhiu, and the Acting Principal of the Kenya School of Law, Mr. Jackson, to examine the question of post-practical training and to submit a report to the Council. I have no doubt that this working committee will examine the different forms which post-practical training has taken and is taking in other Law Schools in countries which have a common law background. In fact, Mr. Jackson will shortly be travelling to Kampala to review the post-practical training programme recently established at the Uganda Law Development Centre. This type of visit, together with a review of a number of

41

papers compiled on the subject, will enable the Council of Legal Education to complete a comprehensive review of the subject and to make its recommendation to the government. Only then will a final decision be made. I emphasize the latter point so as to forestall a battery of questions from loquacious law students.

However, let me say this about the new post-practical training programme. Without prejudice to the final decision made by the government, I would expect to see emphasis placed on the application of the substantive law of which the graduate had acquired knowledge with perhaps particular attention paid to the role of the advocate in private practice, for example, the preparation of documents connected with the transfer of land; the preparation of documents connected with the formation of a limited company; the drawing up of a will; preparing a civil and criminal case for trial; preparing a case for appeal, the organisation of an advocate's office in private practice, practical exercises in accounts. These, of course, are only my own ideas, but the pattern is fairly clear.

Let me now return to the second question I posed. The question of exemption from the examinations of the Council of Legal Education. Now you will not expect me to usurp the powers of the Council in this respect. I must first of all take refuge in reiterating regulation 18 of the Advocates (Admission) Regulations:-

"A person seeking admission under Section 12 of the Act may be granted exemption from such subjects in the examination as, in the opinion of the Council, have been sufficiently covered by him in obtaining any of the qualifications specified in sub-section (1) of that Section, provided that this regulation shall not affect the power of the Council, under sub-section (2) of that section, to grant exemption for any other reasons".

You may, of course, ask what all this means. Well, if you come to the Council already armed with a prescribed law degree, for example, a law degree of the University of Nairobi, the Council will look at the subjects which you have covered in your law degree and these will be compared with the subjects found in the examination of the Council of Legal Education.

In the past it has tended to work out on a subject-for-subject basis. This has often left an applicant with exemption from all examinations save Accounts, Conveyancing, Professional Ethics and Practice. Again, in the past two years the Council has relaxed its requirements by subjecting all applicants to a viva-voce type of examination.

This I understand has been on a trial basis and the indications are that it may be coming to an end. Of course, the University graduates who started their education at the Kenya School of Law will have passed the Council's examination in Accounts, so they may sigh with relief. I am accustomed to hearing complaints from law graduates who have to study Accounts. But, if only you knew the nature of many of the complainants which reached the Disciplinary Committee of the Law Society, your complaints would be muted.

Looking further still into the future I would like to say a few words about opportunities for lawyers in Government services and in other sections of employment. You will appreciate that my chambers employ most lawyers in the service of Government. A variety of legal posts at varying grades are to be found in my chambers, including the Department of the Registrar-General. In the Judicial Department there are posts for Registrars and Resident Magistrates. The Ministry of Lands and Settlement is another department which carries several posts for lawyers. This is a vast field from which the young lawyer interested in Government service has a wide choice. I sometimes wish we could attract more locally qualified lawyers into Government legal services and that once they were there they would remain in the service.

The rewards are there for those who have proven ability, the capacity for sustained hard work and the virtue of loyalty. But these rewards have to be earned and they do not come to those who are content to wait and let things come to them, instead of striving for the prizes which lie ahead. I have had many young African lawyers in my chambers, some of whom are mere birds of passage, here today, gone tomorrow. Money, I suppose, tends to be the counter-attraction here. But, I would like to remind all the citizen lawyers of tomorrow assembled here this evening, to appreciate the fact that their legal education is financed by the government. You are part of our future and the government is entitled to expect some return on their investment. Some of you, I am not sure how many, are bonded to the government on completion of your legal education. Such bonding is the result of a government policy decision and its application is clear to you all.

But, so far as the locally qualified lawyer is concerned, whether he graduated at the Kenya School of Law or the University of Dar-es-Salaam, I have never insisted that the bonded law student should adhere to this bond as far as his future employment is concerned. Neither am I saying tonight that I intend to change that policy. I would prefer to leave it to a moral obligation rather than a legal one.

In private practice the racial imbalance is slowly being corrected. I cannot give you a firm fixture, but there are now African lawyers in private practice (several with their own practices) in Nairobi, Mombasa, Thika, Nakuru, Kitale, Eldoret, Kericho and Kisumu; their numbers will grow through the government's Africanisation Programme. Times have indeed changed.

Opportunities for lawyers are also to be found in Local Government, teaching, commerce and industry (including banking).

Just digressing for a moment, might I say how delighted I am to know that so many attractive ladies will be joining the ranks of the legal profession sometime in the future. I am not at all sure that if I put the clock back, my days in the Bachelors Club would be numbered. Seriously though, in a predominantly male profession, it is not easy for the female lawyer to succeed. We have four female Resident Magistrates at the moment, two in private practice, and there are two in my chambers. So, ladies, do not despair. But, gentlemen, be on your guard, the female invasion of the legal profession is just round the corner.

To return to the general theme, you will find no employment problem in the legal profession. Rather the reverse. There is keen competition for your employment and I find myself having to compete with others for your services. But, this is a healthy sign. The future is yours, it is now up to you to make the most of the facilities and opportunities which the government has placed at your disposal.

I was sent to Thika for my pupillage under the famous lawyer Mr. S. P. Punja, Advocate, who has become a very close friend of mine. I got a house and lived with a friend called Maina in Section II of Thika Town. Unfortunately, until then I had not learned much about women. When my friends and I went rioting in town, I had to learn the hard way how to handle women. In the process, I got entangled with one old lady who almost drove me mad. She taught me many bad things and it is in Thika that I fathered my first child, a daughter. When I went back to the School of Law early in 1972, I left with good memories about the town and I made a resolution that after school I would come back to Thika for legal practice.

We did our final examination in 1972 and I passed all the other subjects save the eighth where I got 49½. Eventually the problem of the eighth subject was solved. Finally, I and other five friends were admitted as Advocates of the High Court of Kenya by the Chief Justice, Sir James Wicks.

Chapter Four

JOINING POLITICS

After admission, I went straight to private practice. I opened an office in Thika near Mongo Hotel. Fortunately, Mr. Murimi and Mbogo, very famous lawyers in Thika then, moved to Nairobi. Also Charles Mwihia, a friend of mine who was then practising at Murang'a, left the Murang'a office to me. I became very busy almost immediately with two offices.

I did well in both offices. In 1980, I acted for Dr. Julius Gikonyo Kiano who had filed a petition against Mr. Kenneth Matiba to whom he had lost the Mbiri seat in the 1979 elections. We were led by Mr. Swaraj Singh. After apparently winning the petition during oral argument, we lost it when the judgement was delivered. We were convinced that the case had been interfered with. It was the only judgement that I knew which was adjourned in the middle. Well, when we came back we lost the petition. I really got confused. Instead of driving to Thika, I drove towards Embakasi. When I arrived at my home in Thika, I went straight to bed because of the disappointment. However, I received a lot of publicity then due to this case. Also so far, Dr. Kiano remains my biggest client.

I really do not know at what point I joined politics. I think I had always been a politician. Politics always excited me from early days. During Dr. Kiano's campaign in Murang'a in 1958, I always went to Kangema to hear him speak and see his Black American wife. Dr. Kiano was a threat to all the police officers at Kangema Police Station. I was 13 years old then, and yet I thought there was something magical about politics.

When Kenyatta replaced Kariuki Njiiri as one of our members of Parliament for Murang'a, I attended all his meetings at Gitugi Trading Centre in Kangema Division. He was a great leader. I liked him and his powerful voice, so I followed him wherever he went in Murang'a. Even today, he still remains my political hero in African politics alongside Kwame Nkrumah of Ghana and Julius Nyerere of Tanzania. I think the three are the greatest African leaders to date.

In 1974, I began to undertake serious political activities when I supported and campaigned for Muturi Kigano in Kangema division elections. I was a speaker in every major political meeting for his campaign. Unfortunately, we lost to Kamotho by only a few votes.

I hoped that one day, I would contest a parliamentary seat. Actually, I set 1984 as the year I would run for elections after, as I thought then, I was professionally well settled. However, events were faster than I had planned. God had it in store for me that I would start politics early. So one evening in 1979, I was sitting in my house at Section IX Thika with my wife and our three little children, Njeri, Irungu and Muthoni. The then District Officer for Thika Mr. Mutherero, came and called me outside. He told me that he needed my short autobiography for use by the provincial administration for the nomination of councillors. That night, I noted all the details he wanted as I rested in my house which I had rented from Hezekiah Mwangi Gicheru a friend of mine and a long standing Deputy Clerk of Thika Municipality. It is in the same house that I married my very beautiful wife Agnes the daughter of a famous Nyeri farmer Mr. Kanyoro. We had also been blessed with five children, the last two being Kanyoro and little Wairimu named after my sister Wairimu.

The following morning, the D.O. collected the information. He in effect informed me that the government had asked for several names for nomination and if I was lucky, I would be nominated. Sure enough, I was nominated councillor and in 1980 I was sworn in.

After the nomination I was called to the District Commissioner's Office at Kiambu where I met the DC Mr. Kabugi. He told me that the government had bestowed on me a very great honour by nominating me as a councillor, and that I was expected to act at all times as directed by the District Commissioner. I thanked him and requested him to inform the government of my most sincere gratitude. He said he would do so, but before I left he directed me to vote for Peter Kibicha when the elections for the Mayor came around because Kibicha was the government candidate. I told him I would decide what to do. I went back to my office in Thika and took the Local Government Act. I went through it but found no directive requiring nominated councillors to vote in any way except as they pleased. So I decided I would vote for Mundia as Mayor because I knew him better than Kibicha. Besides, he was also a better client of mine than Kibicha. Also he was the most intelligent Mayor Thika had had that far. I voted for Mundia but he lost to Kibicha with two votes.

When the votes were scrutinised carefully, it was found out that I had voted for Mundia instead of Kibicha. I do not know how this exactly happened, but I was discovered. Later I was reliably informed that some CID officers assisted in the exercise.

When the year elapsed, we had to elect Chairman and Deputy Mayor of Thika. My group nominated me to run for the post of the Deputy Mayor against the incumbent Mr. George Thuo. Unfortunately I lost to Mr. Thuo with two votes. I felt very sad. However, I was now in politics and that was only my first political fight to lose.

It was at this time that the other group led by the Mayor himself started working for my denomination. Before long, I received a letter from the Minister informing me of my denomination, a copy of which is reproduced here below. I really got disappointed because I had done nothing wrong.

Ministry of Local Government
P.O. Box 30004
NAIROBI

Mr. Samuel Karuga Wandai
Municipal Council of Thika
P.O. Box 240
THIKA

Ref: No. C/1211. III/66   26th August, 1980.

Dear Sir,

NOMINATION OF COUNCILLOR BY THE MINISTER FOR LOCAL GOVERNMENT

I am directed to inform you that due to some unavoidable circumstances, the Hon. Minister for Local Government has regrettably revoked your nomination as a councillor to the Municipal Council of Thika which was published under the Kenya Gazette No. 101 of 11th January, 1980.

P. WAITETE
FOR: PERMANENT SECRETARY AND
DIRECTOR OF LOCAL GOVERNMENT
ELECTIONS

c.c. District Commissioner The Town Clerk
  KIAMBU   Municipal Council of Thika
           P.O. Box 240
           THIKA

50

After receiving the above letter, I wrote a very long letter to my fellow colleagues to bid them farewell. I gave every councillor a copy of the letter which read as follows:

Dear ...

I have received a letter from the Minister for Local Government denominating me from Thika Municipal Council.

As my fellow councillors, I thought it was only proper to inform you about it since there is no scheduled meeting where I can do it. I thought I must do it in writing.

After receiving the letter, I made my personal investigation as to who may have so maliciously misinformed the Minister about me and my investigation revealed that His Worship the Mayor **Peter Kibicha** using his Nairobi contact managed to have my denomination done.

It is an extremely sad thing that a man of councillor Kibicha's personal integrity, intelligence and maturity would decide to use his very important contact in Nairobi for destructive ends. I personally held him very highly for his brilliance and sense of judgment, but now it appears to me that I had not known him well. Politics being what it is, I must say he has done a very sad thing.

I personally do not believe in the politics of undermining others. I do not believe that a leader should adopt such cowardly tactics. I believe in open fight within the framework of democracy. It is very sad that the weapon that I do not believe in has been used to destroy me.

However, I feel extremely proud that I have been able to make some contributions to the Council within the 8 months I have been a councillor. I feel also extremely satisfied that the letter which denominates me does not mention anything wrong that I have done.

Truly, my conscience remains absolutely clean and clear. Since I received the letter, I have been wondering what would be the probable reason that prompted them to work for my denomination except that I stood against his deputy in the last deputy mayoral election and that he would like to have an extra-vote for keeping Councillor Allan Ndachi as Chairman of Finance. But is it not my legal right to stand for the elections? The Chairman of Finance Committee, Councillor Allan Ndachi, is nominated. Why did he stand for election of a Chairman? Councillor Allan Ndachi has been a deputy Mayor even though he has always been nominated. Then what have I done?

I am particularly worried because of the false allegations told to the Minister about me so that he could accept to denominate me. It was unfair because I was not given an opportunity to defend myself. For this reason alone, I will make an appointment to see the Minister at least to seek the reasons and try to defend myself. I am even at a loss because I don't know how to explain my denomination to the people of Thika.

Why should the Mayor adopt the game of elimination? Why doesn't he play an open game? I am extremely surprised. However, God will do His will. As the saying goes, *those who kill by the sword are also killed with the sword*.

Anyway, the purpose of this note to you my fellow councillors was just to inform you of what has happened to me. I must inform you that I loved to be with you and to work with you. I have had wonderful experiences with all of you and I will really miss them but I must say that it is extremely unfair to fight an innocent man out of the Council to fulfil personal ends.

May God Bless You All.

Yours sincerely,

KARUGA WANDAI
A D V O C A T E

After my fellow councillors had received my letter, they convened a meeting at Mr. Mundia's school office to discuss my denomination. Those present were Mr. Mundia, the late Councillor Andrew Mungai popularly known as Kamenu, George Hiuhu, a very close friend of mine, Councillor Ng'ang'a and others. We discussed the matter and it was resolved that my denomination meant one of our group members had been victimised. Such denomination therefore constituted political intrigue by the other group aimed at minimising our number. We saw Hon. Ngengi Muigai at his house in Nairobi and it was decided that we should write an open letter to the Minister copied to all the newspapers and magazines. The work was left to me as a lawyer and the most educated among the councillors then. I went into my house, locked myself up and wrote an open memorandum to the Minister. It was signed by all the councillors supporting me. Fortunately, it was well covered by the *Weekly Review, The Nation* and *The Standard*. I think it is of interest to reproduce here the open letter to the Minister then.

26th September, 1980.

To: Hon. Stanley Oloitiptip Esq.,
Minister for Local Government,
P.O. Box 30004,
NAIROBI.

Dear Sir,

REF: AN OPEN LETTER TO YOU OF PROTEST AND DISSATISFACTION

This letter by the undersigned elected councillors is to register our protest and indeed deep concern and dissatisfaction in the manner in which the affairs of Thika Municipal Council have been handled before and after your visit to Thika on Friday the 26th September, 1980.

The undersigned councillors being **seven** out of the **twelve** elected councillors would like to appeal to you Mr. Minister to review and reconsider the decision you made on the affairs of the Municipality. We would like to humbly inform you of our view regarding what we think are the root causes of the problem and disunity prevalent in the Municipality and which threatens to poison the whole community in Thika.

1. We feel that the nomination of councillors was done in a most irregular manner. Indeed, we know for certain that the particular councillors nominated were nominated for the sole purpose of ensuring that the Mayoral Election of the present Councillor Peter Kibicha was successful. To us the most influential person in nomination of a councillor is

the District Commissioner for the area. It is a well known fact that the previous District Commissioner for Kiambu Mr. M. Kabugi was heavily involved in a partisan manner both in Parliamentary and Civic Elections in Gatûndu Constituency. The people of Thika knew where his sympathy lay.

2. Mr. Minister, the usual practice is to nominate councillors such that they represent the different interests in the community. As you know the community in Thika is composed of women, especially market women, factory workers, industrial traders and different ethnic groups, such as Luos, Kambas and Luhyas.

In view of this fact, the nominated Councillors in Thika today are not justified because they are far from meeting the above requirement.

3. Indeed, three of the nominated councillors virtually come from the same locality, namely Councillor Allan Ndachi, Mrs. Thendu and Titus Muiruri Ndoge. Secondly, both Allan Ndachi and Ndoge worked in the same company at the time of their nomination, namely Kenya Canners. Additionally, Mrs. Thendu works and lives outside Thika and she has no interest whatsoever in Thika Township. We feel that at least the different ethnic groups should have been represented in the nomination.

4. Mr. Minister, it is the normal practice and in accordance with the law under Section 26 c (II) of the Local Government Act Chapter 265, Laws of Kenya that the number of nominated councillors should not be more than one third of the elected councillors.

In Thika there are **TWELVE** elected councillors and **SIX** nominated councillors. Mr. Minister, we believe that when the law was made, it was to make sure that the voice of the elected councillors would never be drowned by that of the nominated councillors. This is particularly so when nominated councillors are nominated not for the purpose of representing the community as above described. This principle of representation is indeed central to our democractic system of government. The two aspects of nomination of councillors discussed above are the roots of problems in Thika Municipality. Anything that is done to justify the above situation only aggravates the situation. Indeed unless this situation is corrected, we do not see an end to the present problems.

5. The above undesirable situation has created a very unfortunate state of confusion which is continuously exploited by the Mayor and his clique ever since the Parliament by-election through to general election, election of the Mayor and his clique and has promoted the very unfortunate view that there are leaders who are not wanted by the government and those who are wanted by the government. Indeed and to our great dismay your visit to Thika and your speech have now been turned into a weapon by these people against us and our member of Parliament.

6. We shall not go into all the propaganda generated by your visit but you must see our frustration. It is obvious that the good will that you called for is not forthcoming from the Mayor and his clique. Therefore, Mr. Minister, your visit to Thika did not solve the problem as you anticipated but indeed worsened the situation because it was quite clear from your speech that you came purposely to protect the evils done by the Mayor and trying all you could to impose

him on us even when he was unwanted. We do not feel that you should seem to contribute in the humiliation and insult which we are subjected to. It is obvious to us that the majority which the Mayor enjoys in the Council was solely created by the manner of nomination and the number of nominated councillors will always be used to humiliate us as elected councillors and frustrate our work. To us the denomination of Karuga Wandai is a perpetuation of this intrigue designed to cater for the personal position of certain individuals in the council and especially the Mayor and the Deputy Mayor. It has been used very effectively by themselves to consolidate their powers and to intimidate other councillors, and let it not be forgotten that Karuga Wandai's *denomination* was sparked off by the fact that he stood against the Deputy Mayor in accordance with the law and indeed within his constitutional rights. If the denomination of Mr. Karuga did not come about as a result of his candidature it is unfortunate that the Mayor and his clique have undertaken a vigorous campaign to make it seem so.

It is a well known fact that Karuga was re-instated through a letter written by the Permanent Secretary in the Ministry of Local Government with instructions from the Office of the President, and addressed to the District Commissioner in Kiambu and copied to the Town Clerk in Thika and the Controller of State House, but this letter never reached Mr. Karuga. We would be most grateful Mr. Minister if you can let us know what happened to such re-instatement and where Mr. Karuga's letter was intercepted. Why this happened we do not know.

Besides all this, we applied for permission from the local District Officer to demonstrate against the Minister for Local Government for denominating me. The fight was so intensified that the Minister for Local Government himself, Honourable Stanley Oloitiptip had to come to Thika and the councillors were to meet him at the main road. I still thought I was a councillor and so I also went to the main road to meet my Minister. He greeted me alongside other councillors. Then we proceeded to the Town Hall but I was followed by the *askaris* and barred from entering either the Council Chamber or the public gallery. Since I did not know what their instructions were, nor did I want to cause any havoc or allow myself to be physically molested, I went to my office to await the results of the debate. My group fought for me very hard. Mundia and Hon. Ngengi fought hard but the Minister could not give in. I was informed his parting shot was: "I am a Maasai. Even if I am circumcised for the second time, that boy will never come back to the Council", and so he ended the meeting.

I went further and saw Hon. Kamotho, a very good friend of mine and at the time a very powerful Government Minister in charge of Higher Education. Fortunately for me, I sincerely had not done anything wrong against the Government and Mr. Musila, the then Provincial Commissioner, Central Province, also supported my case for re-instatement. Pioneer politicians fought for me too, including Dr. Kiano himself.

One afternoon the Deputy Town Clerk of Thika Municipal Council Mr. Hezekiah Mwangi called my office. He told me that he had received a telephone call from Nairobi and that he had been instructed to get a letter from a certain Under Secretary. He told me he would get the letter at Safari Park Hotel. Since he suspected it concerned my re-instatement, he advised me that I should go with him. However, he cautioned me not to say who I was when we got there. So we went in the Council Mercedez Benz and got the letter. After the officer left, we opened it.

The letter read:

> Ministry of Local Government
> P.O. Box 30004
> NAIROBI

Ref: No. C/1211/III/102

Mr. Samuel Karuga Wandai
Municipal Council of Thika
P.O. Box 240
THIKA

Dear Sir,

NOMINATION OF COUNCILLOR

I am pleased to inform you that the Hon. Minister for
Local Government has nominated you as a Councillor
to Municipal Council of Thika. This nomination is
effected from the 14th November, 1980. Please signify
whether or not you accept this appointment.

P. WAITETE
DEPUTY DIRECTOR LOCAL
GOVERNMENT ELECTIONS

c.c. District Commissioner
KIAMBU

The Town Clerk
Municipal Council of Thika
P.O. Box 240
THIKA.

I had been re-instated in the Council! We drank a few beers to the good news. Afterwards I rushed to Thika to tell my people and my fellow council supporters of the good news. We assembled at Gikeno Bar and Restaurant, my political headquarters, and really celebrated.

I remained a councillor until 1983 when the councils were dissolved for General Elections. This time I had decided to be elected to avoid further denomination.

Chapter Five

THE ROAD TO PRISON

I did not get employed by anyone after my admission as an advocate of the High Court of Kenya. Instead I opened up my own practice in an office behind Mongo Bar in Thika. I also took over Mr. Mwihia Advocate's office in Murang'a which he had left after Mr. Murimi and Mr. Mbongo left for Nairobi. So I became busy almost immediately.

I became what one would call a general practitioner. I dealt with all kinds of legal matters. I did both civil and criminal cases. Civil work involved a lot of land cases. My office being in the rural areas, it was inevitable that the bulk of my work came from people in the countryside whose problems mainly revolved around land. I also had a lot of work on divorce and defamation. I was also able to do some election petitions. And there were some criminal cases.

My practice was successful and had made me quite comfortable socially. I had two cars and I was living in Section Nine, an area exclusively inhabited by Asians during the colonial era.

I should say Dr. Julius G. Kiano's petition against Kenneth Matiba is one of the most notable cases that I handled during my practice. It was very revealing. I was able to see for myself the politics of high places. Dr. Kiano was a Minister in the Government before he was defeated by Matiba and his connections were high. As the only African lawyer in his team, he used me more often when making his contacts. I had also been nominated a councillor and so I was learning the art of politics very well.

61

After we lost this petition, I grew a stage further in my political awareness. I was now able to see practically what injustice looked like. In my view, we should have won the petition. How the judges reached the conclusion that we had lost the petition is still a mystery to me. When I was handling Dr. Kiano's petition, I was also approached to act for Mr. Ng'ethe in his petition against George Mwicigi with regard to the Kandara parliamentary election. After we lost Dr. Kiano's petition I withdrew from Mr. Waweru's petition.

I was able as an advocate to go to India to attend the International Bar Association meeting in New Delhi. Our delegation which included Paul Muite, Kirumba Mwaura, Kibicho, Amos Wako and Lawrence Mwaura was led by Mr. Lee Muthoga. For the first time I was able to participate in an international conference. Mrs. Indira Gandhi, the then Indian Prime Minister, opened the meeting for us. I was able to meet other lawyers from Nigeria, Australia, Canada and Britain itself. It was a very rewarding experience indeed.

When my workload both as an advocate and as councillor became quite large, I employed an assistant advocate, Mr. Mungai Kamotho, now deceased.

I acted for several land buying companies. The years between 1977 and 1980 saw the famous coffee boom period and there was a lot of money in the country. There were also very many land buying companies coming up to buy the former European farms. I acted for Gitamaiyu Land Buying Company, Gakenia, Umoja Land Buying Company and Kimunye Investments Company Limited.

Kimunye Investments was the brainchild of Jacob Mwangi Kimani who was then a good friend of mine and a political supporter. In fact, he is the gentleman who had introduced me to Dr. Kiano so that I could act for Dr. Kiano in his petition. He is Dr. Kiano's cousin. When he formed the company which was a private company to start with, he did not have a capital outlay. He approached John Gitonga Kihara, a land owner from around Thika, and asked him to sell to him 200 acres for the development of a housing estate. Gitonga did not even ask for a deposit. He first agreed to sell the piece of land to the company. So Kimani devised a very ingenious plan whereby he proposed, in writing, to sub-divide the 200 acres into plots of one eighth of an acre, each of which would sell for 5,000 shillings. He calculated that he stood to make 8,000,000 shillings out of which he would pay Gitonga 3,800,000 shillings. He would have made a fantastic profit if he had not brought "politics" into the deal. He needed a reputable person to sell those plots for him. As a lawyer friend with a successful practice, I was thought fit to do this job for him. Without even informing me, he put posters all over the town announcing that his company was selling plots through my office. When my attention was brought to this notice, I was very annoyed. He however, came personally to see me and was able to persuade me to accept the assignment.

Jacob Mwangi Kimani then brought in John Kihara Gitonga along and an agreement was drawn by me for the sale of 200 acres. I sought the approval of Waruhiu and Muite Advocates who acted for National Bank of Kenya where the property was mortgaged and this agreement was approved provided we could pay to the bank some money as provided for in the agreement.

The response was excellent. People had money and they came in large numbers. The message went around like wildfire and by the time I disagreed with Kimani, my office had collected a sum of 5,734,946 shillings. That was a lot of money, taking into account I acted for about 4 years only. It also transpired that Kimunye Investments Company was also collecting money directly from prospective plot buyers.

On seeing this success, Kimani became very ambitious. He talked with Gitonga who agreed to sell a further 70 acres for 1,260,000 shillings.

After this agreement was entered into they again entered into another agreement whereby he wanted to buy a further 1,000 acres. This confused everything. He authorised payments to Gitonga without now saying to which agreement the payment was in respect of. Payments were no longer made to the National Bank because whatever was collected in a day was paid directly to Gitonga. After this had gone on for a period the bank complained. Kimani seems to have panicked, and to have sought to lay the blame on me. He therefore, started to make consultations with my political enemies.

The matter was further complicated by Gitonga's entering into a new agreement with Gakenia Women's Group Company for the sale of land. These people also made an agreement in my office and paid some deposit. This matter later got mixed up in my trial over the Kimunye deal. The Gakenia Women's Group Company account was completely separate from the Kimunye Investments Company account. They had absolutely nothing to do with each other.

From 1978 to 1982, I collected money for Kimunye Investments and made payments to them as frequently as I was instructed to do so by Jacob Mwangi Kimani. During the same period I made payments on behalf of Kimunye Investments to Gitonga for deposits against the sale of 200 acres, as per the first sales agreement. The total amount paid to

64

Gitonga in this period was 5,977,564 shillings.

Things started to go awry when after improper instructions to make payments I formally indicated my withdrawal from acting for the company and therefore presented my accounts to Jacob Kimani. He was clearly shocked by the accounts for he was under the impression that I was still holding substantial amounts of money for his company. He had told his directors, some of them semi-illiterate, that I was still holding a good amount of money for the company. Now there was hardly anything left. Kimani ordered that I stop any further collections for his company. Then he stopped coming to my office.

And then there were frightening rumours that I would soon be arrested.

On the day of my arrest, I was to stand best man to a friend of mine, Kimani Nguku, who was renewing his marriage. My wife Agnes was to be the best woman. I woke up early as usual and dressed up. As I did all that, I felt terribly uneasy. The week preceding that Saturday, there was a rumour circulating in Thika bars that Jacob Kimani had arranged for my arrest with the Kiambu CIDs after I had issued a letter to all members of his company explaining to them how I had spent their money. I had written the letter upon being informed by most of the members that they were never informed of the accounts. So to counteract my information, Kimani thought the best strategy was to have me imprisoned. After dressing, my wife and I left for Nguku's home. The whole day I was feeling very uneasy.

Indeed I sensed that something terrible would happen to me, but I did not know what it was. So I brushed this feeling aside and busied myself with the activities of the wedding.

As we settled down for dinner with our visitors, my

brother-in-law, Mr. Mathenge, called me out. He informed me that the Thika CID boss Mr. Mugweru had instructions to arrest me and take me to Kiambu Police Station, where I would be remanded until Monday when I could write my statement in relation to a complaint lodged against me by Kimunye Investments Company. He told me that Mugweru had already left a message to that effect in my house which he was visiting hourly. On hearing this, my fears were confirmed and I knew why I had been feeling uneasy the whole day. I called a few friends of mine and told them what was about to befall me. It was agreed that it was unfair for me to be arrested on Saturday and thus be kept in remand until Monday. So friends would help me get out of Thika, at least for the weekend. I called my wife and our two children who were with us, Njeri and Irungu. I told her what had happened and that I was in a problem. I requested her to keep calm and not to display any emotion over the problem. I was to escape, but she would be given a lift by one of my friends to Thika. I had my faithful driver with me Mr. Paul Kamau Kinu popularly known as *Hiti* (hyena) because of his capacity of hard work and also *Kojak* because of the way he used to cut his hair. I told him there was a major problem and we were to go away. At that time, it had already started raining. I had my Mercedes Benz car with me which was very heavy. However, we managed. We travelled all the way to Nairobi avoiding the main road. I went to my friends' house Hon. J.J. Kamotho, the Minister of Higher Education, but I did not find him there. I was told by the guards that the family had left for home. Although it was about 2 a.m., we had to travel to Murang'a. We travelled through Thika main road and when I saw the town I really felt sad. These CID people were making my life very difficult for a crime I never committed.

We went past Gacharageini right to the Minister's house. Of course everyone was asleep because it was about 5 a.m. so nobody opened the gate for us. Early in the morning someone however did open the gate and we managed then, to have some sleep.

I saw the Minister and explained my problem. He proved a real friend when he told me not to worry because we would go to Nairobi on Sunday evening so that on Monday he would ring a few people and have the matter sorted out. This time I travelled in his car. Of course with the National Flag on it, no one would dare stop it. We went to his house at Kileleshwa and his nice and kind wife organised a room for me. He tried his best on Monday and for a few days things were cool. I rang my office and I was told two CID officers had been stationed outside to await my arrival. Perhaps I should also mention that immediately I left Nguku's house, two CID officers came to collect me but were told I had already left.

Eventually, the Minister advised I could now return to Kiambu and nobody would harass me as threatened. He told me I should give an explanation and the police would investigate the case in the normal way. I was so happy for the concern he had shown over my problem. He asked Mr. Maina, a Senior Enforcement Officer with Nairobi City Council who was a former Police Officer, to accompany me to Kiambu.

We travelled in the Minister's car and on reaching Kiambu, we found Mr. Kiama already waiting for me. Of course he had already cooled down and he told us he was busy then. So we decided to go for lunch and come again in the afternoon. When we came back, Maina left me after he was satisfied harassment had ceased. I was given CID officers to escort me to my Thika office to collect the files concerning

Kimunye. I was then still a councillor and so when I was brought to Thika many people crowded in front of my office. I took all the relevant files to Kiambu and Kiama ordered I be taken home until the following day when I would come and make a statement. I was dropped at my house in Thika and there I was extremely happy to join my family again after a week on the run.

I reported to Kiambu Police Station the following morning and I was given my files to write a statement.

My statement, which I later produced in court read as follows:

> It is true that I acted for M/S. Kimunye Investments Company during the material time.

> Accounts were taken by my office and M/S. Kimunye Investments Company for all the monies received by my office on their behalf on the total sum agreed which was shs. 5,734,946/- and this final figure was agreed and signed for by Isaac Mwangi for Kimunye Investments Company got a copy of the agreed figure sheet while my office retained the original which now is marked 1 in my file number 81/675. This total was arrived at after taking into account all receipts from the company members who pushed the plots in our office and which receipts are contained in the individual files of the members. In addition this figure also includes Shs. 783,366/- which was paid directly to our office by the company.

> Of the above sum the payment on behalf of the company was as follows:

> (a) shs 300,000/- as payment for the first agreement of 200 acres which is marked II in my file number 82TI.

(b) shs. 916,000/- was the deposit paid for the second agreement, receipt of which is acknowledged on the agreement now marked III in my file number 83TI.

(c) As stated in the company's letter dated 24th April, 1981 I supplied to the company a total of miscellaneous payment totalling shs. 2,408,560.40. The letter is marked in my file No. 667/82 as No. IV. The list is also in file No. 675/181 and marked V. I also supplied them with a statement of acknowledgement of receipts signed by Mr. Gitonga the vendor and witnessed by my clerk Alfonse Mulu Muia for the said amount which also indicated earlier payment in the two agreements. The payments were treated as further receipts of the two agreements entered in before.

Gitonga however had disputed acknowledgement No. 1 on the list, on the ground that it was included in the second agreement payment of 916,000/- but after checking the date of the agreement it was found that the agreement dates 5th June 1979 and the payment was on 5th June and the agreement acknowledged earlier receipts and therefore this could not have been included in the earlier agreement. After that explanation there were no more questions either from the company or Gitonga as per the said letter marked IV the total payment to Gitonga was 5,977,564/-.

There were no complaints at all from the company that time except now when I hear that they are now complaining. The payment was made as instructed by the company's Managing Director Mr. Kimani sometimes orally and sometimes in writing but mostly orally. What now happened is that when Gitonga wanted money he would see Kimani and Kimani would either ring me or come with Gitonga.

If there would be available cash, Gitonga would take. If no cash, I would issue a cheque payable to him. At that time we were collecting quite a lot of money so there was no problem. If as you see from page I of the list some of the payments were made in respect of Gitonga's debts, personal debts or hospital fees. There was further payment of shs. 498,000/- as per list supplied to the company and marked VI in my file number T81/675 and supporting voucher in file No. T81/431 in the envelope marked VIII. The costs of the two in the first two agreements was shs. 5,060,000/- that is 1,260,000/- plus 3,800,000/- and whatever balance which was above the amount was to be a deposit for the 1000 acres which was to be bought from Gitonga to make a total of 1270 acres in all.

I also paid on behalf of the company 305,180/- as indicated more particularly on my list marked VI on file No. 687/81. As regards my fees the same was agreed by the company in a supplementary agreement dated 25th May, 1982 when the company made an attempt to recruit me again as their lawyer after I had withdrawn the said agreement marked VIII. It is not possible for the company now to dispute my fees after agreeing to it. In fact if I continued acting for them after 25/5/82 then I would have been entitled to 2% of the total collection. I also paid to the bank shs. 800,000/- as per company's letter dated 25/5/81 marked IX in my file No. 3717/79.

The purchase of additional 100 acres originally was mentioned in the company's letter dated 27th July, 1979 which is marked X in file No. 79/3717 whereby the company paid shs. 400,000/- to Mr. Gitonga as per that letter outside my office in my letter to them dated 30th July 1979. I then drew their attention for the need to follow the procedure of the said letter marked XI in my file number 3717.

Obviously I was dealing with very difficult clients. The problem of the company has always been management. With the greatest respect, the managing director does not possess the required know-how to run a company of that magnitude and complexity. The entire board was also semi-illiterate. Therefore, it was difficult to advise the company. The vendor is also a man of great persuasion and could do anything to persuade the company whenever he mentioned some money so:

(a) There were difficulties in advising my clients. They did not take my advice seriously.

(b) They refused to deposit further monies in my office for payment to Waruhiu & Muite and relied on the money collected from me for all kinds of payments.

(c) Realising that the company has problems then they wait to use me as the scape-goat. The question really is what happened to the money the company collected for all that period?

(d) The payment even then could not be properly done because of these frequent requests for payment to Gitonga and too for these two purchases of 70 and 1000 acres even before the first agreement was completed.

I am therefore denying having stolen Shs. 5,008,946/-

being the property of Kimunye Investments Company. I dealt with the company's money as explained above and as from the accounts supplied to the company.

SAMUEL KARUGA WANDAI
23/4/83
11.15 a.m.

SUPPLEMENTARY

The employee M/S Mungai Kamotho to account from me shs. 2,099,442 this that sum of your subject.

KARUGA WANDAI

Kiama read the statement and he appeared surprised. I thought as an experienced Police Officer he believed me fully but before he could say anything to me I think he had to make some consultations somewhere. He told me to come the following day.

When I came, he said we would instead meet in Thika that afternoon. He seemed very furious then. He was with Kimani the complainant. He shouted at me and told me I had lied and that he was going to formally charge me. He instructed his officers at Thika Police Station to take my fingerprints for him as he went for lunch with Kimani. So when he came back, he asked if his officers had finished with me. They said they had. He put me on the back seat of his CID car and told me we were now going to Kiambu.

On the way to Kiambu, I pleaded with Kiama that I was

innocent and that he should drop me at my house but he said I would know that he was the CID boss in Kiambu and truly, I was to know he was the CID boss. It was really annoying to know that a police officer could use his powers to harass an innocent person if he chose to do so.

On reaching Kiambu, Kiama left me outside the station while he went in to do some work. He then called me into the office and started loading his pistol. He no doubt wanted to impress upon me that he was the real boss and certainly he was. He informed me about the seriousness of the charge that I had to face. I might have to go to jail for seven years. I told him that I was an advocate of ten years' standing and therefore I knew my rights. In any case my conscience was clear; I had not stolen anybody's Shs. 4,000,000. Eventually, he told me to go home. He would call me when he needed me, he said. It was already very late and there was no direct transport from Kiambu to Thika. I had left my car in Thika because I had come in a CID car. I stood outside the police station thinking on what to do when Kiama came out and offered me a lift to Thika, as he was going to Murang'a. I said I would take his lift although I had some fear that he may do something serious like kill me since he had earlier loaded his gun in my presence. However, all my fears were proved wrong when he dropped me right in Thika. I thanked him most sincerely. For the first time, he had behaved like a gentleman.

The matter almost ended there until elections were announced and I decided to run for the civic elections instead of waiting to be nominated. Being nominated was very unsafe because I would not have wanted to go through what I had experienced earlier on when I was denominated.

One morning in August 1983, I was sleeping in my country

73

house at Gaitega Scheme, Kiharu Division of Murang'a District. I was alone since I had left my wife and children at Thika. The managing clerk of my Murang'a office, Mr. Raphael Njuguna, came to my house. After awakening me they showed me the *Kenya Times* newspaper of that morning. It was plainly printed in block letters *"The Riddle of Missing Millions."* The story stated: Karuga Wandai had stolen Shs. 4,000,000/- belonging to Messrs. Kimunye Investments Company since he had failed to explain what had happened to these monies. Kiambu Police Station had confirmed that investigations were going on. I reproduce here below in full the *Kenya Times* story.

RIDDLE OF THE MISSING MILLIONS

A total of shs. 4,084,000/- which was collected from the members of public by a former Thika councillor on behalf of Kimunye Investments Company Ltd. is missing.

And now Kiambu KANU Branch has come under fire from the Company Management for clearing the former councillor for the Thika Municipality elections although the matter has been reported to the authorities.

Disclosing this to the *Kenya Times* yesterday, the Company's Managing Director, Mr. Jacob Kimani, said that the councillor collected the money from the members of the public in 1981 to be spent by Kimunye Investments on buying land for the shareholders but he did not hand over the money to the company.

Documentary evidence made available to *Kenya Times*

showed the Company's Financial Manager, Mr. J.W. Gitau wrote a letter on June 15th this year to the Officer Commanding Kiambu Police Division and copied it to the Kiambu District Commissioner.

The letter said, "The Managing Director of this Company reported a case of misappropriation of shs. 4,084,000/- on April 6, 1983 by the councillor." We shall ask you to advise us when you are likely to take firm action against (him) to enable us to report the matter to our shareholders at a special meeting we are planning to hold in September."

And a letter written by the councillor addressed to the Thika District Officer and copied to the company said in part, "By a copy of this letter we are asking Kimunye Investments to withdraw their complaint with the police or other authorities in the meantime until the accounts are finalised by accountants from both sides.

An auditor's report for the year ending 31 December last year said: In our opinion books have been kept and the accounts comply with the requirements of the Company Act. The amounts shown as deposit have been mainly received by the collecting advocate to the company and the advocate account with the company has not fully agreed between the two parties. We are unable to confirm deposit and advocate balances.

Kimani accused the former councillor of giving lame excuse for the delay to return the money to the company. Members are now demanding to know where the money is, he said.

A police spokesman in Kiambu yesterday confirmed that a complaint has already been filed in connection with the missing cash, and that the matter has been taken over by the C.I.D. for investigations which are almost complete.

After reading the newspaper story, I dressed quickly and left for my office. After telephoning a few friends and finishing with the clerk, I left for Thika. I called my friend Patrick Kamau then popularly called "PH" after the letters of his car's registration number. I travelled with him in his car to Nairobi to conceal my identity. I went and saw the sub-editor of the *Kenya Times*. I made a reply to the allegation published about me. However, despite my detailed reply, an inadequate report was made. I knew then that there was a conspiracy by some people in Thika to have me fixed. The headline was only a part of the plan so that Superintendent Kiama would justify my arrest. Indeed from then on Superintendent Kiama hunted for me like a wild beast.

While on this point on how the police handled me both in Kiambu and in Thika before I was finally taken to court, I would like to say something in general about our police force in Kenya. Police officers in Kenya are doing an excellent job in fighting crime. The police as an arm of the government for maintaining law and order is a very effective organ. In fact a country would not be able to run peacefully without the police force.

However, while the majority of the officers in our police force are doing an excellent job, there are some officers who do not care about what the law says. Such officers are responsible for deaths in police cells and they are also responsible for cases of assaults of innocent persons held by them. Not that they do not know the law or that they do not know what they are supposed to do, but they are simply uncaring officers. Such officers give the police force a bad reputation both in Kenya and internationally. Some of them have rightly been charged with murders that they have committed in the pretence that they are executing their duties. It is unfortunate such police officers are tarnishing the good name of our police force in Kenya. More so because the good name is being spoilt by a few corrupt and selfish officers. I think it is the high time the government systematically did away with these careless and notorious officers.

Coming back to my story, on Tuesday the 24th August 1983, I was in my office attending to my clients. By that time, I had already been nominated by Kenya African National Union as a contestant for the Biashara Ward of Thika Municipality Council. So I had all my nomination papers ready and I was set to hand them over to the D.C. Kiambu Mr. Haji on 30th August 1983. As I worked, my managing clerk Alfonce Mulu Muia, now deceased, rang me internally and told me that there were six C.I.D. officers from Kiambu and Thika who wanted to see me. I felt hot all over the body. Time had now come; soon I would be in custody and so I would not be able to present my papers for nomination. I told Muia to allow the officers in. When they came in, I recognised all of them since they were the same officers who had harassed me before. But this time Kiama was not there. He was waiting for me at Thika CID office. I was taken in a CID car where I was put between four CID officers in the rear seat. There I was squeezed badly and I thought Mr. Kiama had instructed the CIDs to mishandle me. I was dropped outside the CID office Thika. By this time word had passed around that I had already been arrested so people had gathered outside the Police Station in Thika. Mr. Kiama must have felt really victorious because he paraded me outside the CID office

77

for everyone to see. He left me there and went to town with some of his officers to enjoy themselves.

At this time, Kiama had become very close to Kimani and they were always together. It was widely remarked that he had also become very close to the Commissioner of Police and so no other officer could order him around. After keeping me in the police station for a long time, he came back from town and ordered me again into the CID car. As before, four CID officers sat with me and squeezed me tightly. Kiama was travelling in his own Peugeot 404 and the CID car was to follow him. My people also followed us in my car. The car passed through Kenyatta Highway in Thika so that everybody could see the thief. We travelled to Kiambu Town and Kiama ordered me to be booked in. I registered everything that I had at the counter. Kamau Patrick, my driver and other friends were there at the counter. Kiama however chased them away.

I removed my shoes and was put in the cell. The askaris at the counter were very friendly indeed. After Kiama left, they called me back from the cell corridors to come and sit with them at the counter.

There was not much work and so we talked for quite sometime with them, if you like, we killed quite a lot of time. Then they changed over and the new ones were very tough. They ordered me to the cell immediately and I was locked up. I found many other inmates though I could not see them well. Some were smoking and others were already snoring loudly. I had not been to a cell before. The furthest I had gone in a Police Station was the counter or Commanding Officer's office to see my clients.

The bare floor was very cold. All other inmates had spread part of the blanket on the floor they lay on while they used the rest of the blanket to cover themselves. There was nothing left and so I had nothing to cover myself with. Luckily I still had my suit on. I tried to use my coat to cover myself. I also tried to sleep near the others so that I could generate some warmth, but the cement was terribly cold. I could not therefore sleep throughout the night. The inmates started discussing what they would say in court the following day and kept on rehearsing it. Of course they did not know that I was a lawyer because if they did they would have sought my advice.

The following morning we were awakened up very early and paraded on the corridor. After we were checked, we were told to wash the corridor. The askari in-charge saw that I was more smartly dressed than the rest, so he ordered me to take the bucket of water and start washing. Unfortunately I had not learnt to call the askari "Afande" when called. So he taught me how to answer to an askari; 'Karuga Wandai— "Ndio Afande"'. This was a good lesson for a beginner.

I was then taken to Kiama's office. He read the charge and asked what I had to say. I said, of course, that I had not stolen anybody's money. He told me that he would now take me to court because I had refused to co-operate earlier. I told him he was the boss and he could do as he pleased. He pressed a bell and other CIDs came. He ordered them to take my fingerprints. I had feared he would order them to beat me but he did not. The people of Thika had now started coming to see me. My wife and my friend Kimani Kang'ethe came right to the place where my fingerprints were being taken. Kiama came out of his office and ordered them out immediately. He was particularly annoyed about my wife to whom he said I was a *mabuthu*, a term used to refer to prisoners to denote their lack of freedom. They were told to meet me in court. They left. I was then escorted to the court. Kiama was already there with Omondi Tunya, the Senior Resident Magistrate of Kiambu who was to hear my case. However, I was convinced that I would somehow get a bond. After all I was a senior advocate of the High Court of Kenya and a councillor as well. So I thought there was no problem.

Mr. Muraguri, a friend of mine, who was then working as a lawyer for me, had already telephoned and arranged with a very reputable lawyer Mr. Timan Njugi, another friend of mine, to lead my defence. There were also several other lawyers willing to act for me.

When the case commenced, Njugi then stood up and said he would appear for me together with Gautama, Muguku, Kembi, Macharia, a Thika lawyer of good standing, and Mr. P.G. Mburu a close friend for a long time.

Mr. Njugi made a brilliant application for my release on bond, but it fell on deaf ears. The magistrate was not moved at all. He was set to refuse me bail so that I would not stand for the elections. Mr. Njugi had informed him that I was a candidate and that I would personally have to present my papers in Kiambu. He made an order that bail had been refused and that the application could be renewed before him on 7th September 1983 when the case would come up for mention. He made a vague order that perhaps I could arrange with the prison authorities to assist me to come to Kiambu for nominations. I was immediately taken to the police cells in the court premises. I knew between then and 7th was the nomination day that was 30th of August 1983. It was very clear to me that the whole game was aimed at barring me from presenting my papers to the District Commissioner in Kiambu. When the order was made, my people came to say goodbye to me. I received very encouraging

words from my wife. She said, *"Keep up Sam, face it like a man"*. When she is concerned about me she always calls me Sam. We had to wait until five o'clock for the van from Industrial Area Prison to come and collect us for custody. My lawyer Mr. Kembi as well as Mburu and Muguku saw me before the prison van arrived.

Kembi told me he had not given up on bail. He still intended to appeal to the High Court against the refusal of bail and indeed he did so. Other friends including several councillors were allowed to see me in the police cells. At about twelve o'clock people left for home and I was left with the prison warders who were very friendly. Someone brought me some lunch, but I could not eat it. I had no appetite. My mind was busy thinking of how unfair the Senior Resident Magistrate had been. I had always thought of Omondi Tunya very highly. At least he should have considered the fact that I was a lawyer like him. Why should he only see me as a politician? As I thought about these things, the prison van came. We were ordered to get into it, two by two, which we did. I had never entered a prison van before. It was a very rough vehicle with very hard forms upon which the prisoners would sit if one was lucky to get a place. It was overcrowded with the warders sitting in front. We moved through Karura Forest to Industrial Area prison where we arrived at about six in the evening.

On arrival, we were ordered out two by two and were led towards a narrow prison gate. There we found a long line of prisoners who had been brought from other courts. Since I did not know what was going on, I decided to ask an inmate who appeared to have been there before and he informed me a search was going on. As I came nearer to the head of the queue, I noted everyone was being stripped naked. Soon my turn came. I was told to take out everything. I took out my coat, my pair of trousers and my shirt, but I was reluctant to take out my underwear. I could not at all understand why I should take out my underwear. What could I really hide in my underwear? The officer was ruthless. He told me to step aside so that those willing to comply with orders could do so. Just as I was about to do so, the fellow next to me stepped on my toe. I looked up to him to complain but just before I complained, he signalled by his eyes how serious it was to step aside. In fact, by the time I had my eyes on the *askari* once more the fellow had almost taken out his clothes. I dropped my underwear immediately and lifted my arms for inspection. The *askari* then nodded his head. I knew immediately that he had realised I had made the right decision. I later met this prisoner friend in the prison yard. He explained to me that had I stepped aside, I would have been reported to the Senior Officer that I had refused to be inspected and I would have had it.

As the inspection on me continued, I was told to bend down so that my "boot" could be inspected. I complied with the order because the *askari* was not joking. He inspected my bottom very well. The American prisoner would say that his "ass was inspected". I later learnt in prison why prisoners' bottoms were called boots. They are real boots indeed because a lot of booty is hidden there.

After the inspection, we were ordered to go to the prison store to collect our blankets. They were extremely dirty and torn. Each one of them was full of lice. As soon as you held the two blankets in your hands the lice started feeding on you immediately. They must have been quite hungry because the blankets had stayed in the store for some time. As I write these pages I cannot understand the reason why

82

lice are accepted as part of prison life.

After collecting my two blankets, I was then marched to collect my food in the prison yard. It was very badly cooked *ugali*, that is hard porridge and dry beans. I simply could not eat the food. I gave it away to a friendly prisoner who was looking at me hungrily. Another prisoner pulled me aside and told me that I should eat the food. He advised me that in about one month, I would cry for more. Of course I did not believe him then.

After supper, I was taken to a cell named D2 for newcomers and was handed over to the ward charge. He informed me of the sleeping arrangements. I had to start from the toilets until I reached the corner. Sleeping at the corner in prison is like sleeping in a self-contained suite at Hilton Hotel. So I took my place next to the toilet. It was so near the toilet that the water from the toilet was seeping into my blankets. Moreover, the stench was unbearable. People were moving to and from the toilet every minute. Some were having diarrhoea while making terrible noises with their bottoms similar to that of a Sten-gun. I felt so sick, only the previous night I had slept in my double bed next to my wife in full warmth, now I had to accept that this prison corner was my double bed. I cursed Omondi Tunya bitterly with all my heart.

Fortunately, one of the inmates who had been in custody for six months had recognised me. I had appeared for him while in my Murang'a office in a criminal matter. I saw him talking to the charges but I did not know he was pleading on my behalf. The charge approached me and asked whether my name was Karuga Wandai. I said it was. He ordered me to pick up my blankets and follow him. The other prisoners started murmuring that there was favouritism. The charge told them to keep quiet. They did so immediately. I was taken next to the gentleman who had interceded on my behalf but I did not know him. He told me who he was. I realised what I had done for him and dimly recalled who he was. I was very grateful to him. We prepared my blankets in the prison style which he taught me. The cell was too crowded and too hot and since I still had my suit on, I could not sleep. Moreover, the lice were just too many; they had by now gone inside my long hair and it was really terrible. The charge called for prayers which were led by a Christian. He prayed very well to Jesus and God. I felt the prayers were quite appropriate there. Indeed there is also a God for criminals as well, even the thieves and murderers belonged to God. Even me who had supposedly stolen four million shillings belonged to God. He was a merciful and kind God. I also thanked him in my own words. I could not sleep the whole night. Morning came. Mornings were preceded by three furious bells meant for the warders not the prisoners.

Maize flour porridge was served at about 6 a.m. It was badly cooked. I took a little of it and again gave it away.

At about 10 a.m. my people came to see me starting with my wife and friends. My best man Gakanya Maina, his wife Apophiah, Mr. and Mrs. Waiganjo, Mr. Kabui, Kimani Kang'ethe, George Hiuhu and many others came to see me. My mother too, was not left behind. As soon as she knew I was in prison, she also came. For the first time, I realised what freedom meant. I talked to my people through wires and I could hardly see them. My niece Grace Wairimu, now married to Mr. Mathai, came too. She was allowed to see me in the company of my mother and Mrs. Gakanya. Upon seeing me, she started crying. I too started crying. It was terrible. We all cried like little babies. I still recall that time whenever I remember about prison.

When night came, I went to my cell and slept. The following morning we were supposed to see the doctor. He was not a doctor as such, but a Medical Assistant. He impressed me as a medical functionary who would not be acceptable in any institution in the free world. He looked like a drunkard. His hands were visibly trembling. All of us, however, went through his small office. The prescription was identical for all prisoners; an injection to prevent general diseases.

We were then informed that those who wished to see the Commandant should have their names written down. I had mine written down because I wanted to know whether I could be taken to Kiambu for purposes of nomination in the civic elections. To see a Commandant in prison is like seeing the President in freedom. We were taught how to march there, two by two, how to answer him and how to speak and in what language. You must refer to him as *afande* at all times. When my turn came, I stood at attention and explained my case in English. I said: Sir, I am a candidate for Thika Municipal Council elections. I have already been cleared by the ruling party KANU. I am now therefore eligible for election. I am supposed to personally present my papers to the District Commissioner Kiambu, Mr. Haji, before twelve o'clock on 30th August, 1983." "Do you have a copy of the Court Order?". "No Sir." "Then we cannot help you. Tell your lawyers to bring the order."

I was pulled away by the warders and that was that. I was taken back to the cells.

Someone in prison had advised me to work out my way so that I could be moved to Block B. This was because Block B was not as crowded as D2 which was for newcomers. In D2 numbers increased everyday with new arrivals from the courts. I took his advice and soon I organised to be moved to Block B where the number was steady. I had now learnt a bit of prison life. I was of course the only advocate among the criminals. I was also a nominated councillor. My case had also appeared in the newspapers and so I became a notable prisoner. Even some officers started enquiring about my whereabouts when I was moved to Block B. To my surprise, Block B was worse off than D2. Prisoners fought often; indeed any time of the day. I spent one night there and decided that, I would organise to be moved back to Block D2. But before I could do so, a surprise search was launched at 6 a.m. on the morning of 29th August even before we had taken our porridge. We were ordered to strip ourselves naked and then we were searched everywhere. After the search, it was not possible to trace where our blankets were because they had been mixed up.

Among us was one prisoner who was genuinely sick with malaria. Since the medical assistant didn't treat him after complaints, the warder accused him of feigning sickness. They stripped him naked, beat him badly and mocked him. I really felt sorry for him.

After the search ended, we collected our clothes and went out for our porridge. Thank God that was my last night as a remanded prisoner. However, my release did not come about until 10 p.m. that night. By that time, I had managed to go to Block D2. Meanwhile the lawyers were battling with my application for bail in the High Court. Although Mr. Chunga, the prosecutor for the state, opposed it, finally my lawyers managed to get a bond for me. Several friends of mine from Thika and Nairobi stood sureties for me led by Mr. Julius Mwangi, Councillor Kariuki Mbuthia, Kimani Kang'ethe, Waruinge, Wamae, Charles Karanja and many other friends.

My political opponent Mr. Mundia was also there. Of course this was only a cover up since he was one of those behind my persecutions. So the papers were signed late, in fact very late as they did not arrive at the prison until after six. The initial order from prison authorities was that I should not be released until the following morning. But the lawyers were persistent. Mr. Kembi, Mr. Mburu, Mr. Macharia and Mr. Muraguri from my office fought hard. At about 10 p.m. that night, a warder came to my cell. I had already settled to sleep because I had terrible pains from the injection that I had received.

I heard the warder say, *"Karuga Wandai toka mara moja chukua virago vyako vyote uende nyumbani."* ("Karuga Wandai get out with all your belongings and go home".) I could not believe my ears. I collected my coat, put on my shoes ready to go home. Of course before I could go home, I had to go through all the formalities. I found my lawyers and Mr. Kirui, who was the Commissioner of Prisons, waiting for me. When he became the Commissioner of Prisons after Mutua, he visited Kamiti and proved a very effective Commissioner. He seemed to have grasped much about the prison system as he had risen through the ranks. I was sure he was going to be of great use to the prisons' service. On this occasion, he was the one who released me. I came to learn later that he was called in his house by my friends and the prison authorities after my people refused to go home without me. The lawyers also became very obstinate and refused to leave me there. They argued that I had become a free man from the time the bond was signed. So the prison had no right to keep me there any longer. The lawyers succeeded in their insistence and therefore, I was to be freed.

I had already learnt the word "Afande" or Sir, and as Mr. Kariuki explained to me I was now a free man although I would have to appear in court on the mention date, I kept on calling him "Afande" until he reminded me that I was a free man.

I moved out of the prison gates to find a lot of people from Thika waiting for me. My wife and most of my friends were there. These were Joseph Maina Gakanya, Kimani Kang'ethe, Hiuhu, Waiganjo and my relatives including Councillor Kariuki Mbuthia. We embraced each other with Mr. Hiuhu. It was a political victory for me to be released a night before the nomination day which was on 30th August, 1987, that was the following day. I entered into Hiuhu's Volvo and we headed for Thika. I was careful to sit far from the other passengers to avoid infecting them with prison lice. We arrived at Gikeno Bar by which time Mathenge, my brother-in-law, had already organised a goat at my home. So we did not stay long at the bar. Mundia of course followed us to the bar and even managed to come to my house. He told us not to suspect that he was behind my troubles and that he had no intentions whatsoever of causing trouble for me. Well, I left him alone and did not allow him to interfere with my freedom.

At Gikeno Bar, I found many women supporters. They rushed to the car that was carrying me and they all started shedding tears of joy. I too cried like them. We sang one Christian song that was my favourite. Whenever this song is sung, it really touches my heart. Indeed, it sums up my relationship with God my creator. I will reproduce it here. I sang it frequently in prison when conditions became unbearable. When I almost lost the meaning of life the song always infused me with courage. Even now as I write these pages, I believe every word about this song.

Kikuyu

1. Nii ningwenda Ngai, umenyage
    Ningenaga muno niwe
    Tondu niunjikaga wega
    Na ukanyenda hingo ciothe.

2. Irio ciakwa iria ndiaga
    Mai maria nyuaga,
    Ona nguo cia kwihumba
    Ciothe nowe uheaga

3. Muoyo naguo nowe wa'heire
    Niwe ungiragia ngue
    Ungithengia hinya waku
    Ndingiikara gathaa kamwe.

4. We muthenya ona utuku
    Niu'menyagirira wega
    Maitho maku ni mambaraga
    Kuri nduma kana utheri.

5. Ndingihota gukugathira
    Wega waku Mwathani
    No nindakuhoya utumage
    Ngwende muno na nguiguage.

Translation in English

1. I want God to know,
    I am pleased by you
    Because you do good to me
    And you love me always.

2. The food that I eat

89

The water that I drink
Even the clothes that I wear
You give them to me all.

3.   You give me life
You prevent me from dying
If you remove your strength
I cannot survive even
for a minute.

4.   Day and Night
You take care of me
Your eyes watch over me
During the light and
darkness periods.

5.   I cannot be sufficiently grateful
All your goodness Lord
I only pray that you give me power
To love you and be
obedient to you.

On arriving at my house, my wife took my suit and all the
clothes that I was wearing to the bathroom and heaped them
at a corner. Even as she did so, lice spread all over her hands.

I took a quick shower while my friends waited in the sitting
room. We ate meat and I also prepared for the nomination the
following day. Fortunately, I had been cleared by KANU and
all my papers were ready as they had been prepared by Patrick

Kamau who was to become my Chief Campaigner. But as I went to bed the injection that I had been given in prison started taking effect. I started vomiting in bed. My wife called my friend Doctor Wamaitha Kirika (Mrs.) She came with her husband and treated me almost the whole night in my bedroom. I will never forget the devotion of this woman doctor to me. She is a real friend of the family. Later she was to give free medical services to the family. God will no doubt reward her for her good heart. I think she pursued the right profession.

In the morning we moved to Kiambu. My supporters had already organised the followers to come and cheer me up. I felt very sick but I had to go. My friend Ng'ang'a Kamau drove me to the Kiambu DC's office in his Toyota Crown. I handed over my papers to the District Commissioner, Mr. Yusuf Haji. He seemed very happy to see me and wished me well. At the security desk was none other than Superintendent Jeremiah Kamau Kiama. I looked at him and I knew he felt frustrated. I also knew for him the battle was over. For the time being I was well cheered and in the afternoon when we went to pick the symbols, I picked a "KEY" My only approved opponent was Joseph Gachengo popularly known in Thika as *Kameme*. I suppose he is so known because he sells radios.

Chapter Six

ON TRIAL

The campaign took off immediately and I did not have any problems in winning the seat. A lot of lies were spread against me in the campaign. My opponent chose to broadcast about the pending charges preferred against me. His campaigners even threw leaflets to the crowds during my political meetings accusing me of theft but those agents were all arrested and some sent to prison.

When the results were declared, I had won 80% of the votes against my opponent's 20%. I was elected the councillor for Biashara Ward in Thika Municipality. As my election victory was announced by the DC Kiambu, I held my wife's hand very high and we received thunderous cheers from the people. The DC also gave us a congratulatory handshake. We went to Thika and Patrick Kamau, my campaign manager, led the convoy around my ward hooting as a sign of the great joy of my supporters and myself. It was really a moment of great victory. The campaign for the councillorship had ended. It was now time for the next very serious campaign. I had to ask my fellow councillors now to elect me as the Mayor of Thika. I felt I had enough experience of Thika. My opponent was the obvious one, Councillor Douglas Kariuki Mundia. We campaigned well and I think I had a lot of support. I campaigned with George Hiuhu as my Deputy Mayor. Mundia campaigned with Councillor Ng'ang'a Kamau as his Deputy Mayor.

As we campaigned, efforts were made by most Thika leaders to have a united Council. This is because the previous

Council was infected with terrible divisions on the Ngengi/Gakunju lines. Those who supported Ngengi Muigai were one group and those who supported Gakunju were another group. The Council had emerged a predominantly Ngengi Council.

Mundia was then a Ngengi man and so was myself. People argued that we should be able to elect a Mayor and his Deputy without any opposition. I was of this view myself but somehow I knew Mundia was not a vehicle of unity. I felt that if he was given the leadership of the Municipality once again, he would divide Thika on Kiambu/Murang'a lines. So I was determined to fight. I thought time had come to elect progressive leadership devoid of the Kiambu/Murang'a divide.

However, man has not been able to control his destiny. Ngengi Muigai intervened. At the stage when he did so, nominated councillors were already known. He had campaigned to have them nominated and so it was likely they would do his bidding if he requested them to do so. So he spoke to me many times about Thika's unity. He told me Mundia would not agree to be a Deputy Mayor since he was senior in age. I accepted Ngengi's suggestion because I was also for unity. I also felt I was still young and perhaps could try to be the Mayor next time. I thought Ngengi was quite genuine about his approach. I think he was genuinely for one Thika, one Council, one people. At the beginning I thought he was supporting Mundia because he was a Kiambu man but later I got convinced that he was for unity.

So I considered his viewpoint seriously. I think Ngengi and myself were operating on an honest concern for the unity of Thika. But Mundia was not honest. He wanted just to be a Mayor at whatever expense even if he had to cheat. So Ngengi asked me whether I would agree to a conference with Mundia where we could discuss the issue further and I agreed. We decided with Ngengi that we would meet at Ruiru Sports Club. At about 8 p.m. on the appointed day Mundia came and so did Ngengi, Hiuhu and Mbugua. We discussed the matter from about 8 p.m. to about 2 a.m. and I agreed to be a Deputy Mayor. I thought we would really have a united council. It was a very happy moment for Thika if only Mundia lived up to the arrangement because under the arrangement he was to protect me at all times. Little did I know that as soon as he was the Mayor, he would start to fight to have me completely destroyed politically and socially too. Perhaps President Nyerere was right when he said in politics we have only alliances not friends. No doubt Mundia remains the master of Thika politics. At Ruiru Sports Club he managed to manouvre and influence two educated young politicians, an advocate of the High Court of Kenya and a graduate of the world famous Harvard University. That night changed the history of Thika and perhaps my own history as well. For if I had become Mayor, Mundia would not have had an office which he could use to fight me. However, I do not regret now because I think I paid the price for what I believed to be in the best interest of Thika. I am convinced even now that I took the right decision and God will reward me in His own way. So will He reward Ngengi for surely Ngengi is a young politician with political vision. I believe one day he will be a great man.

So the days of election were quite good. Mundia was elected unopposed so were all the three chairmen and myself. Mundia became, "His Worship the Mayor of Thika" for the third time while I became, "His Worship the Deputy Mayor of Thika." The people of Thika were extremely happy. Hon.

94

Ngengi Muigai, Mayor Mundia and Deputy Mayor Karuga Wandai were known to be great friends so Thika would for the first time have unity which everyone desired. For Ngengi, for the people of Thika and for myself, electoral politics had worked out very well. For Mundia, his easy victory was only number one. The next battle had to be waged against me. I very soon realized he would not rest until I was removed from the seat of Deputy Mayor and entirely from the power corridors of Thika Municipal Hall.

Mrs. Mundia, the first wife of Mundia, was proclaimed the Mayoress of Thika. I also proclaimed my wife Agnes Wachera Karuga as the Deputy Mayoress. They were both moved to the Council Chamber with lots of hand clapping. People joked that my wife looked as if she was a daughter of the Mayoress. Indeed that evening was also a very happy moment for me and my friends as we also attended the party for the World Bank Executives at the Hotel Inter-Continental as a Mayor and his Deputy. As we moved through the Kenyatta Highway in the official Mayoral car driven by the Council driver, we felt great. Politics is a game of possibles. Yesterday we could not even have touched this car, today it was our official car. In the absence of the Mayor, I used it several times. Mundia became citizen number one while I became citizen number two in Thika Municipality. We were like a man and his younger brother. I was fully satisfied with my position. Songs were composed in Thika Municipality by the choirs and women groups in our praise. Mundia first and I second. Soon I detected he was not happy about this. He wanted undivided praises for himself. Hence, from the word go, he started rooting me out.

As Deputy I had to renew my office in June the following year. Mundia did not hide his opposition. Despite the

Spirit of Ruiru Club Declaration, he fielded Councillor Ng'ang'a against me. He was sure he would root me out. I campaigned very hard. In the morning of the election, we met face to face at Councillor Tito's house. While I campaigned for myself, he campaigned for Ng'ang'a. I said hello to him and asked him what he was doing at Tito's. He told me he was going to his farm and I laughed. I was with my friend Councillor Simon Wanyoike popularly known as Kihiu Mwiri. We continued campaigning since the elections were in the afternoon. Mundia took the majority of councillors to his house. I met Ngengi at Gatitu Petrol Station in Thika a few minutes to the election. He told me we should surrender if we thought we would lose in the election but I was convinced I would not lose. I was for a united and good progressive Council. Come what may, I trusted my God. God would not allow the plans of an evil man to succeed and destroy our unity. As we waited outside the Council Chamber, the councillors from his house started arriving. They formed a majority of the councillors. But as they passed by me some assured me quietly that although they had been feasting in his house, they still would vote for me. We entered the Chamber Ng'ang'a was proposed and seconded and so was myself.

The two of us moved out of the Chamber. We left fourteen councillors out of the 16 to decide who the Deputy Mayor of Thika would be. As we moved out with Ng'ang'a who was an old friend of mine, we talked about politics. As we waited for the voting, I told Ng'ang'a that politics must be a very interesting game. It makes good friends turn enemies. I told him that, however, we should not become enemies ourselves. Whoever won would serve Thika. As we went on talking, Councillor Mburu came to call us in. Since Councillor Mburu was for Ng'ang'a I felt I must have lost. But on entering, the faces of my supporters showed me that I was the victor. The Mayor was too disappointed even to congratulate me. I did not need his congratulations. I had plenty of congratulations from my councillor friends and others. I felt very happy at defeating Mundia. Of the fourteen councillors that were left in the Chamber, 9 councillors had elected me leaving Ng'ang'a with only 5 councillors. I quickly knew who had voted for him. I had 4 councillors as majority.

Since Mundia had already opposed me and openly supported Ng'ang'a, it was now clear that I commanded the majority of the Council Members. Mundia became genuinely worried about his seat. With nine councillors supporting me, it was clear that when Mayoral elections came around, he would definitely lose his seat to me. Something had to be done to me before the next Mayoral elections. Nevertheless, I stayed as Deputy Mayor the entire year of 1984 after my second victory. The Mayoral elections were not to come until 1985 between June and July.

In between 1984 and 1985 we had united meetings in Ngengi's house. I think Ngengi was genuinely concerned about Mundia's turning against me despite the support Ngengi had given him to become Mayor. I think for the first time Ngengi realised that Mundia was not an honest man; he had taken him for a ride. However despite all that, Ngengi thought he would still control the situation and so on Mundia's request he called us for a goat in his house. The invitation was only extended to the Mayor, the Deputy Mayor, Chairmen of the various Council Committees and the Town Clerk.

We went to Ngengi's house about 2.00 p.m. and had our goat and other food. Ngengi's wife, Wangui, was very kind and she served us well. We all ate well after which we went to

97

another room where we had to hold the discussion. Ngengi was the Chairman.

We discussed some very provocative issues and I think Mundia was angered by the fact that he was found to be at fault by almost every speaker. Councillor Hiuhu, the then Chairman of the Finance Committee, introduced debate on some sensitive financial queries. Before he had gone far, Mundia grabbed a bottle in his hand and hit Hiuhu on the face. Hiuhu was very lucky because he was not hit on the wrong place on the head for he would have died. The whole meeting became plunged in a mess. We took Hiuhu to Nairobi Hospital where he was treated. He made a complaint to Nairobi Police and prosecution followed. For causing grievous bodily harm, he was fined only 6,000/-.

My case at Kiambu never gave me any serious concern. I had already discussed the case with my lawyer Mr. Kembi and other lawyer friends. I knew as a lawyer that conviction was not possible given the evidence. I had not stolen any money. Indeed I had given a full account of how the money was paid so the case went on very well. Apparently, the trial magistrate also gave us an extremely fair hearing.

In fact he made me so comfortable in court that I felt he was bound to be just and fair and that I had nothing to fear. At the close of the prosecution's case, my lawyer Mr. Kembi, gave a brilliant submission of no case to answer. I thought the magistrate had no alternative but to acquit me. But on the day of the ruling, I was put on my defence. I could not believe it nor could my lawyer and friends. Now I started feeling uncertain about the judgement and I felt quite unsafe and uncertain. Maybe the magistrate was going to convict me anyway. I thought he could not because, at least, there must be some shred of evidence. He would not convict me on nothing. So I was given the date of my defence. I did not want to call my witnesses. However I did not take any chances. So I gave a sworn statement and accounted with supporting documents for every penny I had received. I was cross-examined by the prosecutor and I think his cross-examination made my case even stronger. Once again, I gained courage. I thought I would now go free. The date of judgement was given as 17th April 1985: The election for the Mayor of Thika was by then three months away. So I went home with my wife and the few friends who had come to court.

We had to wait until 17th April 1985 for Mr. Jacob Ombonya's judgement. On the 17th April at about 10.00 a.m. the judgement was delivered in open court as required under law by Jacob Ombonya the Senior Resident Magistrate, Kiambu.

I spent the day before the judgement which was a Tuesday in my office. I stayed in my office the whole day. I saw my clients as usual and nothing really looked or appeared unusual. After about 5.00 p.m., I went home to be with my wife and children. I had advised my mother not to travel from Murang'a to Thika but she had already come to my Mamboromoko house in Thika with my sister Wairimu. Llyod Mugo, a very close friend of mine, also came to see me. We all had supper together.

When Mugo had left, I put on the security lights and walked around the compound. I started becoming anxious and a sudden fear seized me. I did not know what to do. Life seemed to be entering into a cloud. However, I convinced myself that it was only because of the pending judgement and I should not be afraid. After all, justice would be done. Mr. Jacob Ombonya will ensure justice is done.

I went back into the house and as soon as I sat down my

wife gave me a cup of tea. It is usual for me even now to have a cup of tea before I finally go to bed. As I was taking my tea, the telephone rang. The call was from a fellow councillor, Mburu Mwaura. He told me that I should advise my wife on the things that I thought she would dispose of in case I was imprisoned. I should perhaps advise her which friends she should see in case of my going to jail. I asked him why he was so sure that I was going to be imprisoned.

He told me he was not sure and then remarked that "these days you cannot be sure". I really got worried; I felt very saddened. My eyes could not see well though the lights were on. I finally told him I did not need to tell my wife what to do. If I was imprisoned, she would know what to do.

I took Councillor Mburu's call seriously because he was not only Mundia's good friend but also his greatest political supporter. I got disturbed. However, I did not tell my wife about the call. I tried to call a close friend but his number was engaged.

When Ombonya put me to my defence there were rumours that my political opponents had already seen him and they had been assured that he would do the needful. These rumours were spread more widely by Jacob Kimani, the complainant company's chairman. I could not help thinking that Councillor Mburu was telling me they were already assured that I was really going in. What was interesting is that Councillor Mburu seemed to know that I would go in for five years. It was very sad indeed. Judgements are supposed to be pronounced only after mitigation is done.

Superintendent Kiama was seen a few days before judgement in the company of Mundia and Kimani. He was very frequent in Thika. So what Mburu told me may have been the assurance already given to the three gentlemen. Well, I tried to sleep that night but I could not. I did not touch my wife.

In the morning I quietly prayed to my God for courage. When I got dressed, my wife kissed me on the cheeks and she wished me well. I was very pleased with her encouragement. Another gentleman friend of mine, Mr. Ben Ngara, had also come from Murang'a. So in the morning we all prepared to go to Kiambu. Before I drove to Kiambu, I once again went round my home compound. I looked at my mango trees, my two cows and my he-goats and they all looked fine.

In my care was my wife, my mother, my sister Wairimu and my friend Ben Ngara. I drove my Mercedez Benz KQE 598. I loved it.

I drove fast through Mamboromoko road into Thika-Nairobi highway to Ruiru Town and finally Kiambu. We did not talk much. On arrival at Kiambu, I found that many friends were already there. I found Superintendent Kiama with his Deputy Chief Inspector Mugweru waiting for me. I parked the car. I did not even wait for my passengers to get out. I did not even see them get out. I hurried to court number one. I passed Kiama and his Deputy and said good morning to them. They immediately followed me to the court. It was hard to go to the dock. There were so many people who had crowded the court.

Most of my friends had found their way in and the court was fully packed. I saw the Thika Town Clerk, Mr. Wamwangi, already seated. Councillor Mrs. Kaba, Councillor Hiuhu, Councillor Muriuki, Councillor Wanyoike, Mr. Kiiru Karuga (my step brother), Joseph Gakanya Maina (my best man), Mr. Ngwatha, the new Kiambu County Council Chairman and many other friends. Superintendent Kiama had already taken his position at the bar.

My lawyer Kembi, and his partner Mr. Muhia were already

seated and so were several other lawyers who had come for their own cases. Jacob Kimani, prosecution witness number one and the chairman and Managing Director of the complainant company were already in court.

I went straight to the dock. The court was not doing any other business then. I folded my arms and then Mr. Ombonya started delivering judgement. I was composed. I was intact, I was solid, I was ready, I was not afraid. As he read the first paragraph it was all clear; it was a question of how many years. He did not even start the judgement at the beginning. He started on the page where he had reasoned, if one would call that reasoning, why I should be sent to prison. The faces of my friends started getting dark particularly those who understood English. I refused to lose my stature and composure. I followed his judgement to the end. It read as follows:

The accused Samuel Karuga Wandai is charged with stealing by agent contrary to section 283 (C) Penal Code. He pleaded *not guilty*. Kagai Prosecution Witness 1—(PW1) an employee of the firm of M/S. Waruhiu & Muite told the court that M/S Waruhiu & Muite Advocates are the lawyers for National Bank of Kenya. On 21/12/78 an agreement was entered into between the National Bank of Kenya as charges and Kimunye Investments Company for sale of a piece of land No. 280/3 at Thika (EXI). The Vendor was the National Bank of Kenya and one Kihara Gitonga and the purchaser was Kimunye Investments Company Limited. The accused was the Advocate for the purchasers Kimunye Investments Company. Shs. 300,000/- was to be paid to the vendors on execution of the agreement and Shs. 750,000/- was to be paid on completion. The purchase price was to be paid to the vendors

M/S Waruhiu & Muite Advocates. Only Shs. 800,000/-
was paid by the purchaser to the Vendor's lawyers and
nothing more. The agreement (EXI) was not completed as the conditions were not fulfilled.

Jacob (PW2) a Managing Director of Kimunye
Investments Company testified that his company had
among its objectives the purchase of land for its
members. The accused was the company lawyer. The
company asked the accused for a land to purchase. The
accused got land for the company for purchase in Thika.
The vendors of the piece of land were M/S. National
Bank of Kenya and one Gitonga Kihara. The piece of
land had been charged to National Bank of Kenya for a
loan to Gitonga Kihara who defaulted and the Bank was
selling the land to recover the loan to Gitonga Kihara.

The company entered into an agreement to buy the land
for Shs. 3,800,000/- with the accused as its lawyer and
M/S. Waruhiu Advocates as lawyers for the Bank
(vendor). The accused collected money from members
of the company who paid Shs. 5,000/- per plot of the
land and Shs. 200/- for accused fees. Each member of
the company who paid was given a plot number. All the
money collected by the accused was to be paid to M/S.
Waruhiu & Muite Advocates for National Bank of
Kenya. The accused had collected Shs. 5,734,946/- as at
16/3/82. The accused paid Shs. 800,000/- from this
amount to M/S. Waruhiu & Muite Advocates for the
National Bank. It was agreed in the agreement that Shs.
1,750,000/- would be paid for the release of the title deed
of the land to the company. The accused paid only Shs.
800,000/-. On this discovery the accused was stopped
from making any further collections from members
effective from 22/3/82 and was stopped from acting for

the company. The matter was then reported to the D.O. The National Bank of Kenya then advertised to auction the land as it had not been paid. The accused was supposed to pay the purchase price to M/S. Waruhiu & Muite Advocates only. He was not authorised to pay any money to Gitonga, the charger of the land.

Gitonga (PW3) testified that in 1978 he entered into an agreement to sell a piece of land to Kimunye Investments through his lawyers M/S. Waruhiu & Muite Advocates and the accused was the lawyer for Kimunye Investments. There was an agreement drawn up by the accused and M/S. Waruhiu & Muite Advocates. He was not to be paid through his lawyers who were also the lawyers for National Bank of Kenya. He was to be paid Shs. 300,000/- from the purchase price and the rest was to be paid to the National Bank of Kenya. The accused paid his Shs. 300,000/- only and no more. The accused further paid Shs. 800,000/- to National Bank of Kenya through M/S. Waruhiu & Muite Advocates. He did not receive any other money from the accused. His loan with the National Bank of Kenya is still outstanding. The accused was his lawyer in another matter.

Daniel (PW4) testified that he is a member of Kimunye Investments Company and was in 1978 and 1981 a Director of the company. The accused was the company lawyer. The company entered into an agreement to buy land. The piece of land to be bought was charged to National Bank of Kenya. The accused did not pay for the land deposits money from members of the company for this purpose.

Joseph (PW5) a financial manager of Kimunye Investments Company told the court that the company was to purchase a piece of land through the accused. The land was charged to National Bank of Kenya. The accused collected money from shareholders. The accused paid Shs. 800,000/- towards the purchase and Shs. 300,000/- to Gitonga (PW3).

The accused had collected the money from members but did not pay the Bank. The Bank decided to auction the land for payment. The Bank is still claiming payment.

Peterson (PW6) testified that he is a member of Kimunye Investments Company. He had paid Shs. 5,000/- to the accused for purchase of land. The accused was the lawyer for the company. There was no land which was bought.

John (PW7) testified that he is a member of Kimunye Investments Company and he had paid to the accused Shs. 2,800/- towards purchase of a piece of land. There was no land bought.

Arthur (PW8) testified that he is also a member of Kimunye Investments Company. He had paid Shs. 1,200/- to the accused for the purchase of a piece of land. He has not been allocated with any land to-date.

Isaac Mwangi (PW9) told the court that he was an employee of Kimunye Investments Company as an accounts clerk. The accused who was the company lawyer had collected Shs. 5,734,946/-. He prepared the trial balance of the company as at 30/6/82. The trial balance did not agree with the balance sheet. He does not know why the trial balance does not agree with the balance sheet. There were some irregularities in the accounts of the company.

Gathayia (PW10) told the court that he bought a piece of land from Gitonga (PW3) through his company called Gakenia Women Group. The accused was acting for the company and there was an agreement of sale on 2/7/79. The accused was paid Shs. 350,000/- for the purchase of 1000 acres. Later the piece of land they were to buy was put on sale by the Bank.

Kiama (PW11) a police superintendent investigated the case. He received a complaint from Kimunye Investments Company on 22/3/83 to the effect that the accused had misappropriated over Shs. 4 million while engaged as the company lawyer. He arrested the accused on 22/4/83. The accused made a self-recorded statement under enquiry (EX14). There were two other sale agreements on the 70 and another 1000 acres to Gakenia Women Group. He recovered documents from the accused which assisted him in the investigation.

In his defence the accused stated that he is an advocate of the High Court of Kenya practising under the name of Karuga Wandai & Company Advocates. During the period 1978 to March 1982 he was engaged as counsel to Kimunye Investments Company which was to purchase a piece of land from Gitonga (PW3). He had instructions to collect funds from members of Kimunye Investments Company which he banked in his account for the purpose of purchasing land. He did not have instructions on how he shall disburse the funds. He adopted his statement to the police EX14. He collected Shs. 5,734,946/- from the members of Kimunye Investments Company. He disbursed the money as outlined in his certificate of shareholders (EX5). From the funds collected he paid Shs. 300,000/- to Gitonga (PW3) in respect of the first agreement of sale (EX1). He paid Shs. 916,000/- as a deposit for a second agreement (EX15) and Shs. 800,000/- to National Bank of Kenya. He paid some money directly to Gitonga (PW3) in respect of the 1st agreement (EX1). He made other payments in the course of his work which included the

Commissioner of Lands and recovered his own professional fees. He is a Deputy Mayor of Thika and he had differences with the Managing Director. The land to be purchased was charged to National Bank of Kenya whose lawyers were M/S. Waruhiu & Muite. There was an agreement of sale (EX1) between himself and M/S. Waruhiu & Muite Advocates who were acting for the vendor. The purchase price was to be paid to the vendor's advocates M/S. Waruhiu & Muite Advocates according to the agreement. He paid Shs. 800,000/- only to M/S. Waruhiu & Muite Advocates. His client Kimunye Investments Company did not give him time to accumulate enough money to pay the vendors. The land which was to be bought was advertised for auction on 16/3/82 due to lack of payment to the Bank. There were other agreements between his client Kimunye Investments Company and Gitonga (PW3). He paid some money directly to Gitonga (PW3) on the instructions of his client. It is common ground that the accused was acting as counsel to Kimunye Investments Company in the purchase of land reference No. 280/3 Thika, measuring about 200 acres. The land belonged to Gitonga (PW3) who had charged it to National Bank of Kenya for a loan. He (Gitonga) had defaulted in payment of the loan to the Bank and the Bank was selling the land in the exercise of its power of sale as charged. It was by this exercise of its chargee's power of sale that Kimunye Investments Company Limited was buying a portion of the land for its shareholders (members) and hired the services of the accused as an advocate. It is also not in dispute that there was an agreement of sale entered into between the accused as advocate for the purchaser and M/S. Waruhiu & Muite Advocates for the vendors (EX1). The agreement was made under the Law Society conditions of sale. The sum of Shs. 300,000/- was to be paid on executions of the agreement. This sum was duly paid by the accused.

A further sum of Shs. 1,550,000/- was to be paid to M/S. Waruhiu & Muite Advocates for the vendor John Gitonga (PW3) on completion of the survey but before the sub-division. A further sum of Shs. 1,750,000/- was to be paid to the vendor's advocates on the issue of the sub-division deed plan not later than 31/3/79 and this amount was not to be paid to the vendor's advocates M/S. Waruhiu & Muite Advocates. There was also in the agreement a condition that if for any reason the purchaser fails to complete the sale he shall forfeit a sum of Shs. 95,000/- to the vendor absolutely. It is not disputed that the accused collected money for this purpose from members of the company which he banked in his client's account or name. The sum of shillings 800,000/- only was paid to the vendor's advocates from the collection of Shs. 5,734,946/-. Due to the failure by the accused to pay the money, the National Bank of Kenya advertised to auction the land in question and this was stopped by an injunction filed by Kimunye Investments Company in the High Court suit No. 2928 of 1982 at Nairobi.

It is clear that the accused received the Shs. 5,734,946/- from Kimunye Investments Company for a particular purpose namely to pay the vendor's advocates M/S Waruhiu & Muite Advocates for purchase of the piece of land No. 280/3 at Thika before 31/3/89. This is set out expressly in the agreement (EXI). The accused was under an obligation to deal with the money he collected in a particular way. He might have kept the money in a box or he might have kept it in the account at the Bank as he did, but one way or another, he had to keep the funding in existence for that purpose. The accused stated in his defence that there were subsequent agreements which his client entered into and this complicated the payment. Subsequent agreements must be treated as subsequent agreements. They were to be dealt with after the first agreement if the interests of the accused client were to be catered for. It must not be forgotten that the intentions of Kimunye Investments Company and the vendor's advocates M/S. Waruhiu & Muite were that the accused will collect the money and pay the vendor before 31/3/79 as expressly set out in the agreement (EXI).

Smith and Hogan in their book on Criminal law (3rd Ex) (Butterworths) give an instruction of a similar problem at page 413:

> "If P were to give D £100 with instruction to go to a travel agency to purchase a ticket for a flight, the normal inference would be that D is under an obligation to deal with the £100 in a particular way. In such a case it would normally be clearly envisaged by both parties that D will apply that particular £100 to the purchase of the ticket and not otherwise."

The accused as a lawyer, owed certain duty to his client Kimunye Investments Company. The accused as a lawyer should have exerted his best efforts to ensure that decisions of his client are made only after the client has been informed of relevant considerations. His advice needed not be confined to purely legal considerations. He should have advised his client of the possible effect of each legal alternative. And in the event that the client insisted upon a course of conduct that was contrary to his judgement and advice the accused could have withdrawn from the employment.

At all times the accused in the excercise of his professional judgement should have acted in a manner consistent with the best interests of his client. The accused seems to have abandoned this aspect of his professional responsibility to his client Kimunye

Investments Company who to-date have not acquired any piece of land they have proposed to buy through the accused. The defence by the accused that he was paying the money collected to others at the instructions of his client is clearly untenable and amounts to dishonest appropriation.

The accused was under an obligation to Kimunye Investments Company to retain and deal with the funds collected in accordance with the written agreement (EXI) executed by himself and M/S. Waruhiu & Muite Advocates for the vendor. The accused was under a fiduciary duty with regard to the money to be collected which was earmarked for the fulfilment of the agreement (EXI).

It must be pointed out, however, that Kimunye Investments Company was not on a sound financial management. The evidence of Isaac (PW9) shows that the trial balance (EX D22) which he prepared did not agree with the balance sheet as at 30/6/82 for reasons he does not know. The annual report (EX D3) is bound to be unrealistic. I do not rely on the books of the company as showing its correct financial position. The accused must have taken advantage of this financial maladministration in the company. The audit report (EX 5) is consequently unreliable. The statement of the accused to the police (EX 14) as to how he spent the money collected is also unreliable.

The accused was aware that failure to pay the vendor, the National Bank of Kenya, would have sold the land in question in its exercise of its chargee's power of sale, yet the accused, who is a lawyer, ignored paying the vendor. There can be no other explanation than that the accused misappropriated the funds with the result that he was unable to rescue the land once the National Bank of Kenya advertised it for auction.

Fortunately, Kimunye Investments Company filed an injunction to stop the proposed sale in the High Court Civil case No. 2928/82 at Nairobi. I cannot believe that the accused was oblivious of the consequences of failing to pay the vendor as agreed. The accused who is a Deputy Mayor of Thika was engaged in an election to the Thika Municipal Council at this point in time. This may explain the reason for the misappropriation. I do not see any grounds to hold that the accused is a victim of his political opponents on the Thika Municipal Council elections of that time.

The obligation for the accused to pay the vendor arose from an express agreement (EXI) of which he failed to honour after collecting Shs. 5,734,946/- which was far in excess of what he was supposed to pay the vendor's lawyers M/S. Waruhiu & Muite. If there were other agreements which his client Kimunye Investments Company entered into, these would have been dealt with after the first agreement (EX1) was completed. The company had the freedom to enter into other contracts and this should not be an excuse for failing to honour the first agreement (EX1). And it was the duty of the accused to advise the company accordingly as its lawyer. The accused misappropriated the funds and had looked for excuses and other expenditures to explain how he spent the money avoiding to honour his agreement with the vendor (EX1). I am satisfied that the accused is guilty as charged of stealing by agent contrary to section 283 (C) of the Penal Code and I convict him of that charge.

After convicting me, he then as usual asked for my mitigation. Since my lawyer never expected a conviction, he had not taken my particulars. So he asked for a short adjournment so that he could take my particulars. We moved to the cells area since I was already a convict. As we walked out, I could see that my lawyer, a young man of great courage, had already lost his hope. He was so upset, so surprised and so confused that he did not know what to do. He just asked me whether it was really true. I told him, "Kembi, it is not a daydream, it is true that I have been sent to prison. What now remains is for how long. So please take my particulars." He told me that since I was a lawyer, I should make my mitigation. I told him it was his duty. Then he composed himself and took my particulars. We then went in. He sang the song; my client is 40 years old, married with five children and so on, but he was talking to a rock. Since I was standing high on the dock, I could see his honour take a blank piece of paper to write what Kembi stated in mitigation. After taking note of all that, he never wrote again. His sentence therefore was already written. Kembi's mitigation was not going to change it. He started reading the sentence. "I note that you are a Deputy Mayor of a leading Municipality but the offence is serious". He had even forgotten to write that I should refund the money after the sentence. He later added it so that it would fit in with the requirements of the law.

I was not an advocate of the High Court of Kenya any more, nor His Worship the Deputy Mayor of Thika Municipality, not even the Chairman of my old School Board of Governors, but a convict. A thief of poor people's money. By the stroke of a reckless and unjust pen, my life had been ruined. My practice was destroyed, my family too and my business. Above all, I had now been reduced to a second class citizen. As the warders pulled me out of the dock to start my sentence, I looked up to heaven and tried to see whether I could see my God. I didn't but still I asked Him for courage.

I blamed those who took me to school, those who elected me a Deputy Mayor, those who placed me high. I blamed myself for having left my village Mihuti to come to Thika. Perhaps if I only stayed in my village I would not have got into these problems. I would be a happy villager with a wife and children feeding on whatever came on our way. Just then, I remembered the brave words of my best man who once told me that "Nature is stronger than man." It was meant to be so from the beginning of time.

Five years! That was the time I took to qualify as a lawyer. In five years' time, my eldest daughter Njeri would be 13 years; the youngest Wairimu would be seven. I was forty and I would be forty five. This was a long time indeed, everything was going to change for me. I felt like this was the end of my life and the world.

As I thought about all that, people asked for permission to see me. I was taken to the exit of the court cell and I saw most of my friends waiting there. Mathenge my brother-in-law with all his other brothers, Mama Maria, Lucy Nyambura, Wanjiru Mwangi and my fellow Councillor Hiuhu and many other people were there. I asked to see my mother and she came. She held me very tightly and so did I. Then she said, "*I leave you to God who gave you to me. He will still bring you back to me.*" I told her He would. I felt tears falling from my eyes. This poor woman lost her husband long ago and now will have no one to look after her. In any case, when I finish my sentence in 1990 she may not be alive. She had no other son except myself.

Who would bury her? Anyway I left her to God to do what He wished with her. My wife was allowed in and so was my best man, Maina, and Hiuhu. We talked quite a bit. We discussed with her what she should do. Mama Wangechi, my

113

best man's wife was also there. Mrs. Kihara came later. Mrs. Wangui Mbari, a long time friend of mine from Kangema who was already showing signs of an early pregnancy, joked that when I come out of prison after five years, her new baby will be more than four years old.

Some meat was roasted for me by Councillor Hiuhu Mwiri and other friends. I could not eat much. Little did I know that I would not taste the roasted meat for a long time to come. If I knew, I would have eaten well. My lawyer and friends assured me that they would definitely appeal and that they were to meet immediately to raise money and pay for the appeal.

By two o'clock everybody had left; friends, relatives and sympathizers. I was now left in the hands of the prison warders. They were very friendly. They encouraged me and told me not to worry as this was not the end of life. There were many important people in prison and that I would get used to prison life. I did not believe them then.

I had now known the prison van after my remand in Nairobi Industrial Area Prison and so when it came, I was handcuffed and entered the vehicle to start my five years' jail sentence. A long and dark journey lurked ahead.

Chapter Seven

INSIDE KAMITI PRISON

The prison van that came for us was from the Nairobi Area Prison. My commital warrant was addressed to the officer in-charge of Nairobi Area Prison. We travelled through Nairobi streets to the Nairobi prison. As we passed through those streets, I smelt the air of freedom through the van's wired windows. I envied the free men outside who took freedom for granted.

We arrived at Nairobi Prison at about 6 p.m. We went through the routine check-up and finally we were given our evening ration. I had now known the compound of Nairobi Area Prison but this time I was taken to the prison section which was by far better than the remand section. In fact, prisoners live better than those remanded. Since I was to serve five years in jail, I was only registered temporarily pending my transfer to a major prison. I did not know which prison I would be sent to because I had thought Nairobi prison to be a major prison. I was taken to a cell with six others. I had two blankets and was given a nice corner. I learnt that sleeping at a corner in prison was a privilege. It took days in a cell before one qualified to be at the corner. Later in Kamiti, I had to pay lots of cigarettes to be at the corner.

I did not sleep the whole night. I only picked a few hours sleep in the early hours of the morning, but by 6 a.m. I was woken up so that I could be transferred to the prison that would suit my sentence.

I was taken to the duty officer and I noted some change. When I was there on remand, prisoners were badly beaten but now no one was beaten or harassed. When I enquired, I was told that a new commanding officer who was a saved Christian had replaced the old one. That was very good indeed. When I went to the duty officer, he already knew me. He asked me whether I knew I had made the headline on the *Nation,* and that I was on the front page in both *The Standard* and *Kenya Times.* I said I did not know. He showed me the three newspapers. However, he did not allow me to read them. I pleaded with him to allow me to serve my sentence in his prison but he told me that I could not because his prison did not take sentences over four years. I told him that my people were already organising an appeal and if he only would be kind enough to allow me to stay on until my appeal.

He said it was not possible. I was then called to join the other prisoners who were going to court so that I would be transferred to my prison. I entered the vehicle to Nairobi Law Courts. At the High Court, I was pushed to the basement where the cells are. I really could not understand life. Only a day or two before I was an advocate of this court, and now I was a dishonoured advocate of this court not suitable to address the judges sitting in those courts, but only good enough for the basement beneath their feet. I really cursed the trial magistrate Ombonya for doing this to me. At least he should have respected the fact that I was a lawyer. He should have known that I was an advocate of the High Court of Kenya who had been taught for five years about the meaning of justice and who had practised law for twelve years seeking justice for my clients in courts of law. Well, that was not important now; what was really crucial was my survival in the prison system for the next five years.

116

As I sat in my cell thinking about all this, a warder came to me and asked if I was Karuga Wandai the former Mayor. I had the courage to tell him I was not a former Mayor but I still was one, only that I was a *Mayor in Prison*. He laughed and told me very soon, I would know that I was nothing more than a convict, a criminal. However, he told me someone called John Karuga Kiiru wanted to see me. He asked me whether I knew him and I said yes and that I would like to see him. He came in. He asked me what I needed. I told him I did not mind some milk and a loaf of bread and if possible two Kenyan dailies, *The Standard* and the *Nation*. He was allowed to bring all those items. I had not eaten since the day I was convicted. So I ate the bread and drunk the milk to my full satisfaction. I also read the papers.

At about 12.30 p.m. we were called to board the prison van popularly known as *mariamu*. The warder to whom I was attached was a very kind man. He told me that in Kamiti Prison papers were not allowed and if I did not mind, I could give him the papers so that he could go to read them. I asked him to keep them for me until I left prison. That is what he did. He gave them to me the day after I came out of prison.

I read through them and since I had already made plans to write this story, I kept them too and I think it would be of interest to reproduce the relevant stories here.

The *Daily Nation* ...

DEPUTY MAYOR GETS FIVE YEARS

Thika's Deputy Mayor, Councillor Samuel Karuga Wandai, was yesterday jailed for five years for stealing 4,008,946/- from a land buying company.

The Kiambu Senior Resident Magistrate Mr. Jacob Ombonya, also ordered Wandai to refund the money at the end of prison term.

Senior Sergeant William Chege prosecuting, the defence Ombonya that Wandai (40) was a first offender.

Before the sentence, Mr. Kembi Gitura, the defence counsel, said Wandai was married with five children. Although his client may have been negligent, he had not benefited from the money.

Mr. Ombonya noted that the money collected from shareholders of Kimunye Investments Company totalled more than Shs. 4 million and had not been recovered.

It had been collected from members of the public with shares in the company and entrusted to the Deputy Mayor in his capacity as an advocate, for the purpose of buying land. Mr. Ombonya noted that no land had been bought, adding that none was likely to be bought because the one they had earmarked had been advertised by the National Bank of Kenya for sale to regain a loan advanced in its security. The result is that the shareholders have lost their money as well as land. Wandai is an advocate of the High Court of Kenya and should not have been involved in such a fraud, said Mr. Ombonya.

Mr. Ombonya also noted that Wandai "is a Deputy Mayor of one of the big Municipal Councils of Kenya."

Delivering judgment in a packed Kiambu Court, Mr. Ombonya said an agreement had been entered into between the National Bank of Kenya, as chargees, and members of Kimunye Investments Company for sale of a piece of Thika land from John Kihara Gitonga.

Wandai was the advocate for Kimunye Investments Company shareholders and had collected Shs. 5,734,946/- by March 11, 1982.

He had paid Shs. 800,000/- from the amount to Waruhiu & Muite Advocates for the National Bank of Kenya.

Mr. Ombonya also noted that it had been agreed that Shs. 1,750,000/- was to be paid so that a title deed could be released to the land-buying firm.

Wandai had paid Shs. 800,000/- to the National Bank of Kenya and on discovering this, the accused had stopped any further collection. He had also been stopped from acting for Kimunye Investments Company.

Mr. Ombonya also noted that Wandai had not paid for the land despite having collected money from members of the company.

The Magistrate also noted that Wandai had collected money from the land-buying company but had not paid it to the Bank and the National Bank of Kenya had decided to auction the same land for lack of payment.

"It is common ground that Wandai was acting for Kimunye Investments Company in the purchase of a piece of land charged to the National Bank of Kenya," he said.

Mr. Ombonya also said the land belonged to Mr. Gitonga, who had "defaulted in repayment of the loan to the Bank."

The Standard ...

THIKA DEPUTY MAYOR JAILED

The Deputy Mayor of Thika, Samuel Karuga Wandai, was yesterday jailed by Kiambu Court for five years after he was found guilty of stealing by agent a total of Shs. 4,018,946/- belonging to Kimunye Investments Company Limited.

The Kiambu Senior Resident Magistrate, Mr. Jacob Ombonya, who gave the accused 14 days to appeal, also ordered Wandai to refund the money after completing his prison term.

Immediately after the judgement was delivered, close relatives of the accused broke into tears.

Several women were spotted being helped into waiting cars. *"Ngai wareka ohwo biu"* wailed one of the women, asking God why he let it happen.

Wandai had denied that on divers days between 1978 and March 1982 in Thika Township, being an advocate for Kimunye Investments Company Limited, he stole Shs. 4,018,946/- which he had received from the members to deposit in a local bank.

Mr. Ombonya, treating the accused as a first offender, said that over four million shillings was involved and had not been recovered yet.

The magistrate also said that the money was collected from members of the public who had shares in Kimunye Investments Company for the purpose of buying land which was never bought.

Mr. Ombonya observed that the proposed land had been advertised for sale by auction by the National Bank of Kenya for non-payment of the loan advanced on it as security.

He said the result was that the company members had lost their money as well as land.

He rejected an earlier submission during mitigation by Wandai's lawyer, Mr. Kembi Gitura, that the accused was a victim of his political opponents in the Thika Municipal Council.

Mr. Ombonya said the accused's obligation to pay the settlers arose from an express agreement which he failed to honour after collecting Shs. 5,734,946/- which was far in excess of what he was supposed to pay.

I learned from *The Standard* that when I was imprisoned, many people cried. No wonder when my wife was allowed to see me her eyes were red and swollen.

The vehicle travelled fast to Kamiti. It was escorted by a police nine-nine. I started a conversation with some of the prisoners but I was wearing nicely for them to bother about me. Some were already very contemptuous. "Another rich man has joined us," their countenance seemed to say.

We entered Kamiti Prison first gate and then headed for the second gate. It was opened and we were allowed between the two gates.

The vehicle was inspected and finally we were allowed in. I had visited Kamiti prison before as a student in the Kenya School of Law. I had also seen my clients there, but I could not make head or tail of how it looked like then. Now Kamiti seemed to be a different place altogether. We moved in and the vehicle stopped. The other prisoners knew where to go and so after they were sorted, they moved to their respective blocks. I was told to wait so that I could be documented. I waited in the hot sun gazing at the buildings that would from thence house me for the next five years. After a short while a warder came and called my name. I was pushed to an office so crowded with warders that it never looked like an office.

As I entered there, I was ordered to remove all my clothes. *"Toa nguo zote, tutakupa yetu"* (meaning: take out all your clothes, we shall give you ours). I took off the coat, the trousers, the shirt and the socks. I thought at least I should be left with the underwear. One warder shouted at me loudly, "You fool! Even your underwear. Remember you are not a Mayor here." I wondered how a man could move without his underwear. The warder stood up and started approaching me. I knew things were serious so I complied. I took my underwear off and I remained naked in front of other men with my private parts uncovered. For the first time since my conviction, I realised things were going to be very difficult indeed. It appeared very clearly that it was going to be a terribly rough time. But I was already within the walls of Kamiti Prison and there was nothing I could do now except to remember the precious words of my mother that she had committed me to God. To Him too, I committed myself. I had extreme faith that He would not desert me. He had always helped me before, so why should He desert me now?

After all the particulars were registered, I was told to thumbprint the areas they wanted me to sign. I was informed that according to the prison rules, I could not sign because I was presumed illiterate. I thought I was more educated than any of those warders; I was even more educated than the prison commander. So how could the prison warders presume me illiterate?

Well, that was just a beginning. The entire prison machinery is designed to dehumanise a prisoner and one of the first steps was to treat an educated prisoner as totally illiterate. I learnt later that it was a terrible misfortune to be an educated person in prison.

After registration, the next step was to move to a duty

officer. I was escorted by two warders to him. His name was Mbuthia and, as I was to learn later, he was legendary for his brutality to prisoners. He was really feared. As I entered his office, he shouted at the warders as to why my hair had not been shaved. "I do not like to see the hair of these people," he said. However, Mbuthia was an intelligent officer by prison standards. He ordered the two warders to leave his office and thereafter became very friendly. He had on his desk the *Nation* with me on the headline. "So you are the one we have been waiting for, eh? What happened? You did not come here yesterday after your conviction. You stole Shs. 4,000,000/-? That is a lot of money. Now that you are in prison nobody can penalise you. Tell me sincerely, did you steal the money? Well if you did, you stole intelligently."

He did not even give me a chance to answer any of his questions. When he paused eventually, I told him I had not stolen anybody's money. I told him I was appealing to the High Court. At that point he suddenly became very impatient. He called the warders and told them that I should have my hair shaved immediately. I was consigned to the prison's barber and taken under a tree. My hair, which was part of my personality, was cut. I had not cut it since 1972. For thirteen years, it had been part of me and now it was no more. Truly I was in prison. I had no underwear on my buttocks and my testicles were now hanging under my buttocks like those of an uncastrated he-goat. Now my hair was gone. I thought I was finished. I would never again be His Worship the Deputy Mayor and an advocate of the High Court of Kenya. I was no longer Sam or Karuga Wandai but prisoner Number KM/379/85. The sun was hot. My hair having been cut I really felt the heat. I experienced a severe headache and my head almost burst. A warder decided I should be moved to Block D. In the prison yard, I found Major Ngami and he called out for me. He was, I think, Sergeant but the prison warders liked to be called Majors. I was already carrying my two blankets.

"You come here. What is your name? Why are you imprisoned and for how long?" asked Ngami. When you are new in prison, you answer all these questions. Then he told me that he would call a prisoner who would give me a welcome into the prison. He called a fellow called Muchiri who has since been released. He told Muchiri to give me a blow hard enough to make me fall down. Prisoner Muchiri was really a funny man. I thought he meant it but he was only joking and after seeing how scared I was, he told me I was a coward and he would wait until the following day to give me the blow. When I was six months old in Kamiti, Ngami became very friendly. By this time, I had been promoted to stage three and had replaced the red stripe on my arms' sleeves with a green one. I learned later that Ngami was a very fair warder.

On this first encounter, he released me and I moved in towards Block D. I met many prisoners doing their respective duties. They were all in white and looked like ghosts or persons in limbo waiting to go to hell or heaven anytime. The place looked funny. Somehow, newcomers were already known. Prisoners gazed at me. At Block D, I found another advocate prisoner. He was an advocate I knew for a long time but now he looked different. He, however, recognised me and welcomed me to the prison. He had already been in prison for three months and so he was, at least settled. We talked much and he gave me a lot of courage.

Once in Block D, I was informed that I had to wait for the charge. This is a very important person in prison as he is the fellow in charge of a block or ward. He was also very powerful. Charges were quite harsh to us new prisoners. When he came in the evening, I was introduced to him. I was told to wait until after supper so that he could show me the cell in which I was to live. At about 5 p.m. there was the count *hesabu* in which prisoners were counted more carefully than money. So when the charge shouted, "*hesabu*," one had to squat immediately unless one had a letter from the doctor saying that he could not squat. The *hesabu* had to agree with official figures otherwise we could not go for supper. We knew officers who had their *hesabu* agreeing immediately while others had problems—real and often deliberate, in having the *hesabu* agree.

After *hesabu*, we were given food. It was badly cooked *ugali* with *sukuma wiki*. In fact the vegetables were so bad that most of the leaves were already yellow. I refused to eat or rather I could not eat this kind of food. I still remembered the meat and good food of freedom days.

This food here was unfit for human consumption. I gave it to the prisoner next to me who not only finished his share but also mine. I thought he was a strange human being. How was he able to feed on that kind of food with such relish? Little did I know that later I would swallow saliva when that kind of food appeared before me. The *ugali* would be a delicious cake and the yellow *sukuma* would be like green spinach from City Market. I had to eat this kind of food every day until I left the prison. Surely a human being has many experiences of leisure as well as of suffering. But even under conditions of adversity, men still survive.

After supper we were locked in. I was locked in cell 42 in Block D at Kamiti Maximum Security Prison. It was truly a maximum security prison because even a helicopter could not get me out. There were so many doors one had to pass through before reaching my cell and so many walls that even trying to escape was unimaginable. My first night at Kamiti Prison was really a terrible night.

I was locked up with three other prisoners; one a Maasai and the other two Kambas. All the three were convicts of stock theft. I was a convict of stealing by agent. They were all illiterate. I was so frightened of them that I could hardly sleep. In the cell there were four small plastic buckets for our use for both short and long calls. My fellow prisoners were un-reasonable because they made me sleep next to the buckets. I however managed to face my head to the other side of the buckets while my legs faced the buckets. Immediately the bell rang for sleeping time, the three fell asleep. They did not even talk to me. I tried to talk to them in Kiswahili about the prison life, but they refused to talk. At the duty office, I had been warned as a newcomer to be aware of homosexuals. I really did not know whether the three gentlemen sleeping in the same cell with me could be homosexuals.

If they were, then I was very unlucky because if all three turned against me and each had a go at me, I would surely have died. This morbid fear kept me awake almost the whole night. I prepared my two blankets and tried to sit down. As I struggled, the three inmates were already snoring. I could not understand how they could really sleep so comfortably in these hard conditions and start snoring. I stood up and looked through the small holes in the cell where the warder checked the prisoners. There was a small light coming from the direction of the watchtower. I looked outside and this light gave me some hope in life. At least I was not dead. This light must be coming from life. I stayed awake until around 5 a.m. when the first prison bell was rang. We were not ready to wake up. I tried to sleep at that time but I could not. So at 6 a.m. we were counted. We all stood up against the wall facing the door. The officer counted us and in about 5 minutes time, the doors were opened.

We then had to carry the urine downstairs. Fortunately, no one had gone for a long call. We moved downstairs, poured the urine in a sink and then washed the buckets with stagnant water.

The ordinary toilets were already full even in the morning. We continued using them nonetheless. One had to be careful not to have the faeces smeared on his buttocks. In fact, we had to lift our penises with our hands otherwise they would penetrate the faeces. I could not believe this. The condition of the toilets in Kamiti was so bad that I felt sure I could not survive under such conditions. It was just too unhealthy. But to the warders, it looked normal. As we struggled with all these difficult conditions, they just pushed us and ordered us to eat our porridge.

One could not have a shower at all; in fact we had to wash our face with the little drinking water provided in cups. I did not have any water myself, so I did not wash my face. The porridge was really bad, and to make it even worse, it was not well cooked. I could not drink mine. I gave it to the prisoner next to me. Moreover, we drunk the porridge as we squatted. It was very hard, but those who were used found it easy. When time for cleaning the cups came, all those who were employed and had working cards were counted and told to move out. Those not employed were left behind and told to clean the cups. As we cleaned the cups, I looked at the walls surrounding us. Surely, man must be an animal. Even the lions in the zoo do not have such high walls around them. The walls were so high that the government must have spent a lot of money building them. That was not all, because there was yet another wall surrounding the whole prison.

During the day, things were a bit better. At least I could argue with some University students and with my lawyer friend as we worked.

When the employed prisoners returned to the block, one prisoner came to me and told me he hailed from Murang'a, which was my home district, and that he knew me as an advocate. I was very pleased. He asked me whether I had any problems. I told him I had many. My biggest problem was the inmates of my cell. I did not feel safe. He told me he was sharing a cell with the deputy block charge who also hailed from Murang'a and after the count, he would introduce me to him. After the count, he did so and the deputy charge was very kind indeed. I told him of my problems with the food. He told me he would try to see that I was given some beans at least. The food suppliers in the kitchen were given a few Roaster cigarettes and I got some beans. I was so hungry and I really enjoyed the beans. At least they were better than *ugali*.

Chapter Eight

FIRST APPEAL

On my third day in prison, I was called to go to see some visitors who had come to see me. Although one had to see his visitors through a hole, I felt encouraged by those who came to see me. I had thought the end of life had come. I was also very pleased when the visitors informed me that my friends were already appealing against the trial magistrate's judgement. The following day, Mr. Kembi came and assured me of the efforts being made by himself and my friends. He also informed me that my friends had agreed that the late S.M. Otieno, a famous criminal lawyer, would lead my appeal. He had asked for a fee of Shs. 50,000/- but after some negotiations, he agreed to do the appeal for Shs. 30,000/-. Already a friend of mine. Mr. Ben Kinyanjui Muigai had paid Shs. 15,000/- to be refunded later. Kembi was preparing the proceedings in Kiambu. I was really encouraged. At least I knew no High Court Judge would support conviction. I thought it was only a matter of days and then I could be free.

My wife also came to see me. She had applied for a special visit which had been granted though I had to see her in the presence of the Prison Commander or a Senior Officer.

Visiting the Prison Commander's office in Kamiti Maximum Security Prison for a prisoner is like visiting the President's office in the free world. One is marched there after being thoroughly inspected. I was marched in and I found my wife there but we could not be left alone. However, I was lucky to be granted a special visit. I had to leave her there and return to my cell. As I left her, I saw pain in her eyes. This was a woman I had shared a bed with and now I was not even allowed to touch her. It was terrible indeed. That is what it meant to be a prisoner.

When I moved back to the block, I was asked who had come to see me. Prisoners are very curious about things happening. I suppose since there is nothing to break the monotony, at least seeing someone is something good.

My friend from Murang'a managed to have me moved from cell 42 to cell 41 where he lived with two other prisoners. One of the prisoners was a court broker who knew me because of my work. Cell 41 was better; there we discussed many things. I learned how Roaster cigarettes were obtained and how they were used as the only means of exchange in prison. They were the only recognised legal tender. All of my cell mates were smokers. They smoked heavily! They even had their special lighters which were carefully hidden in special places where warders could not find them.

When Sunday came, I asked whether people were allowed to go to church. There was a chapel at the gate which was used by all denominations. The Protestants worshipped first and Catholics afterwards. It was really nice to go to church. It was an ordinary church except that it was in prison. The priest came twice a month so some of the mass services were conducted by prisoners. This one in particular was conducted by a long serving prisoner who had been in prison for 16 years for robbery with violence. It was well done. After the mass we moved back to the block. When we were being counted, I saw a fellow I knew in freedom. He had served 3 years in jail and was in his final year. We talked for some time and so I was left behind by the people going to my block. He belonged to Block A which I was told during the colonial days was for Indian and

Arab prisoners. He was an experienced prisoner hence he managed his way through but I could not. I had lots of problems getting to my block. I was questioned a lot by the prison warders until I really got scared.

Then at the gate of Block D I found a warder. He was a very cruel warder who was well known for beating prisoners. The in-charge of the block was there. On seeing me, the in-charge shouted at me that I should forget I was a Mayor. He called me in Kikuyu *"Mugoma uyu"*, meaning "You she-goat." He ordered me to crawl on my knees from where I was to the block. It was a distance of about 50 yards. I tried but I could not make it. My knees were injured and they started bleeding. Since in prison one puts shorts and not trousers, the knees were bare. I think the in-charge wanted me punished because he did not intervene. As I continued struggling, the warder continued insulting me. Fortunately, an in-charge of the cleaners intervened. I think he promised the warder some money. He spoke in the prison language which I could not understand then, but I managed to reach my cell before him. The cells were not locked. Throughout the week I really had problems with my knees. It was long since I had knelt bare. I think the last time I knelt bare was in primary school. That was a long time ago.

The following morning, the dreaded Kamiti Search was conducted in the block. Immediately after the count, we were ordered out naked. It was about 6 a.m. and it was very cold. Prisoners shook like little boys. I really could not understand. Why should the prison authorities do such a thing to us? Why should they order people of different ages and cultural diversity to take off their clothes? At least they should allow them to remain in their shorts. As I pondered these questions, one of the prisoners was being badly kicked by a warder. He vomited blood. Where was one to complain? Maybe the next prisoner to receive kicks would be me. Then I looked at my naked body between several other naked prisoners and felt like life had no meaning. I think I was just like a dead man. A dead man was even better because he did not know what was happening. When the search was over, we were kicked back to our cells to dress. As I looked for my clothes, I genuinely cursed Ombonya. At this time of the day, he must be comfortably sleeping in the government house and here I was, half dead. I felt genuinely bitter but I could do nothing. I stayed unemployed for about two weeks. At this time, I was only doing general duties.

In the third week, I was employed. I was taken to work in the Number Plate Section of Kamiti Prison. It is in Kamiti Prison that all the number plates in Kenya are made. Such activity earns the government a lot of money. The revenue is so substantial that the department alone can run the entire Kamiti Prison including paying staff salaries, yet despite all that work the prisoner is still a useless thing in the eyes of the warders.

I quickly learned how to make the number plates and I was fully employed. Like other prisoners, my salary was ten cents each day. I could not appreciate such pay until Christmas came around. This is the money that is used to buy bread. The officers at the number plates section of the prison were very understanding. It was my first time to know there was a difference between the warders in charge of discipline and those that are teachers. The warders at the number plates section or working places are somewhat kinder than those in other disciplines. Some joined the prison service when they were already technicians and are at least realistic and more progressive.

I also found a lot of changes when I was employed. The prison life became now a routine. We had to wake up at 5 a.m. and have porridge at about 6 a.m. and report to work at about 7 a.m. throughout the week except for weekends. Weekends of course were the most boring, because it meant being locked up for the twenty four hours of the day except during meal times.

I worked in the number plate section for about 4 months and in August, I was moved to the braille section. This section made books for blind people from normal books. It used to be a section of the intellectuals in Kamiti Prison. It was a better section because we were dealing with books for the blind students in secondary schools and for the first time, I was able to read another book except the Bible. I had to be trained and it took four months. I was apprenticed to another prisoner who was really strict. I found another advocate in the section. I also found a senior officer of the disbanded Kenya Air Force and we worked very well indeed. We also shared many of the problems together. In the section, books were plentiful! I read many of the books that were given to us to transcribe. I think I liked the section very much.

Incidentally, this was the only section where there was no warder in-charge. The prisoners were under another prisoner. This prisoner of course was of a senior rank. He was a trustee. Trusteeship in prison is the highest rank a prisoner can attain. Once one becomes a trustee, he can even go outside the prison unguarded. In small prisons, trustees even escort other prisoners to hospital. The other rank close to the trustee is that of stage 4. When I left prison, I had been promoted to stage 4. I was quite a senior prisoner then.

The rank next to stage 4 was stage 3 for the remanded prisoners who were still awaiting trial. Stage 4s were experienced prisoners who had stayed in prison for quite sometime and knew many of the prison tricks. For them it was easy to move from one block to another and also manage to handle the warders. They were experts in smuggling things in and out of prison by using the warders, even the prohibited articles or *marufuku*. So this was really a good stage with quite a number of privileges.

It is in the braille section that I first drunk tea made in prison. I could not believe it but as the English saying goes, "necessity is the mother of invention". Because of difficulties we encountered, prisoners had learned many survival tactics. Water could be boiled in the metal section of the prison at the same time as the warders' water for tea. A cleaner would cleverly bring it to the braille section undetected in return for several cigarettes. Tea leaves and milk powder smuggled into the prison would be used to make tea. Tea tasted very good when we managed to make it. I really do not understand why prisoners are not allowed some tea. It is only a drink and I don't see anything special in it. I think denial of tea is just another way of mistreating prisoners.

During the month of May, my lawyer, Mr. Kembi, came to see me. He told me that my bail pending appeal had been rejected. It had been argued before Mrs. Justice Owuor, the lady judge, and had been unsuccessful. I had high hopes that I could be released on bond pending appeal. I felt that no judge had the right to refuse my application. It appeared I was wrong. My wife, my best man and my step-brother, Mr. Kiiru, came to prison to see me. My wife came crying. I talked to them bravely and told them to go home. We would wait for the appeal patiently.

On or about August 1985, my lawyer came to see me again. He told me that my appeal would now be heard. He told me that it would be heard by Justice Schofield and Mrs. Justice

Owuor. I felt this time justice would be done. I had appeared before the two judges previously and I knew they were quite forthright. Mr. Justice Schofield was trained in England and thus I believed he must be a real child of justice. I believed no Englishman would do injustice because it was a part of English life to do justice. Mrs. Justice Owuor was an experienced woman judge in our country and for that reason, I had faith in her. I had no reason whatsoever to think that she should not do justice. Mr. Otieno, now deceased, was to lead Kembi in the appeal while Mr. Chunga, now Deputy Public Prosecutor or, if you like, Deputy Attorney General, would lead the prosecution. I thought all these people were experienced men of the law who would find Ombonya was wrong and get me out of prison.

I told my lawyer to make sure that I was produced in court to listen to the proceedings and he agreed. However, he never applied for a production order for me to appear in court. Although I gave him a lot of credit for many other deeds in my entire trial, he scored badly in this regard. I wanted to be present and hear the lawyer debate for my liberty. I wanted to see for myself the High Court, our fountain of justice, doing justice and allowing my appeal. Later, he told me that he consulted with Mr. Otieno who led him in the appeal and they saw no need for me to appear in court in torn clothes. Since they were quite sure that I would be released, they thought I should only come out of jail a free man and in my suit. Well, for a person outside prison, this is good logic but for a prisoner a chance to get out of hell is always welcome. I therefore did not manage to witness the first appeal drama. I only describe what I was told by those who came to see me. I was told that my lawyer clashed from the very beginning with the lady judge when he objected to her hearing the appeal because she had heard the application for bail pending appeal. He argued well for the four days that he did so. He argued so well that my friends who were in court were quite sure that my appeal had to be allowed. Mr. Chunga on the other hand argued very strongly for the state. He argued for two days and at the last stages he was even asking for a retrial.

After the arguments were closed, judgement was set for 10th October 1985. Those who came to see me assured me that it was now a question of days for me to go home. I could not sleep properly subsequently. Those were very hard days indeed. I dreamt of my children, I dreamt of my wife, my mother, my property, my Thika house, my friends, my everything. I kept awake and even during the days I never felt sleepy. Some of the educated prisoners who had a chance to read my proceedings kept on assuring me that I would definitely go home. The 10th October came. I expected the judgement to be read in the morning and so I hoped someone would come to pick me up. Morning came and passed. The afternoon came, no word. Night fell, no word! I stayed for a full week without knowing what was really happening. My lawyers did not bother to communicate with me, so I kept on wondering what was happening. It was a very hard time indeed.

After about a week, someone came and told me that my judgement had been adjourned to 18th October 1985. This was Lucy Nyambura, the chairman of Mugumo Women Group that I had helped to form. She was very sure that they would collect me on 18th October 1985 for home. She told me not to worry because I had only a few days to remain in prison. I had no reason to doubt her at all. As a lawyer, I was sure no judge of the High Court would support the judgement of the trial magistrate.

I patiently waited for 18th October 1985. That morning, I was convinced I had taken my last cup of porridge in prison. I had by now managed to move from Block D to Block A and then I had just moved to Block E. I occupied a single cell alone. I waited and nobody came to tell me what was happening.

I started feeling that things were not good. The judgement may again have been postponed or interfered with.

A few minutes before we were closed in our cells, a lawyer friend of mine who was serving a sentence with me came from his lawyer. He did not want to break the news to me but finally he got some courage. He told me that my appeal had been dismissed and it was all in the local press. I could not believe him, yet he had no reason to cheat me. We were immediately locked up again.

In my cell, I started thinking about the misfortune that had befallen me, if what my prisoner friend had told me was true. It meant that I would not leave prison until 1990. I had a long way to go. Surely did the two judges decide to uphold Ombonya's judgement? Someone must have interfered with the judges for surely they could not dismiss my appeal on merit. I tried to sleep but I couldn't. I felt hot all over my body and was sweating. I looked out through the little cell hole to an outside light that was still on. I thought I was really in a grave and all that remained now was for the soil to be heaped on me. I was in a lonely cell. All alone, no wife, no children, no mother, no friend; only myself. Life had become solitary for me, since only me and my God were in the cell. I clearly felt close to my God. I had thought He was being unkind to me, but I was now convinced it was for a big lesson. Indeed, I saw, everything will go one time. Wives will go, children will go, mothers will go but my God and myself will never part. I came into the world naked and I possessed nothing except the life that was in me. There I was in the cell with nothing except the three prison uniforms that were given to me. But even the uniform was not mine. So everything I owned in freedom was no longer mine. I think that was a great moment of personal realisation. That was the moment I realised what life meant. Indeed for the first time, I was able to know the meaning of the famous Biblical words, *"What does it profit a man, if he gains the whole world and suffers loss of his heart?"* What profit was there to own the whole of Nairobi and yet your heart was lost! The heart, not the worldly goods, was the engine of human beings and if the engine ceases, then that signals the end of life.

Yet I was still alive and strong. I could eat, I could drink and sometimes I even had wet dreams. So from that moment, I decided that even if I remained in prison until the end of my days, I would have to do a major service to myself. At any cost, God and myself had to protect my soul and my heart.

The following is the judgement of the High Court of Kenya dismissing my appeal:

"Samuel Karuga Wandai appeals against his conviction by the learned Senior Resident Magistrate, Kiambu, on a charge of stealing by agent, contrary to section 293 (c) of the penal code.

The appellant is an Advocate of the High Court of Kenya and acted for a company called Kimunye Investments Company Ltd. (hereinafter called "Kimunye"). Kimunye wanted to buy some land and PW3 John Gitonga had a plot of land LR 280/3 at Thika for sale. This land had been charged to the National

Bank of Kenya and the bank required the plot to be sold. On the 21st December 1978, the parties entered into an agreement for sale of two hundred acres for Shs. 3.8 million. The agreement for sale is exhibit 1. Shs. 300,000/- was paid to Gitonga on the agreement being entered into. The balance was to be paid through Gitonga's Advocates Messrs. Waruhiu & Muite, Shs. 1,750,000/- on completion of the survey of sub-division and the balance of Shs. 1,750,000/- on the signature of the transfer which, according to the agreement, should not be later than the 31st March 1979.

It was later discovered that the land intended to be purchased was seventy acres larger than the parties to the first agreement thought and so a second agreement, exhibit 15, was entered into for the sale and purchase of this extra seventy acres for a sum of Shs. 1,260,000/-. A deposit of Shs. 916,000/- was paid on that agreement and the balance was to be deposited with the appellant. There was reference to a third agreement of one thousand acres but according to PW3 JACOB MWANGI KIMANI the Managing Director of Kimunye said that the agreement never took off.

Kimunye wanted to purchase the land for its members and invited subscription for plots from its members. Each member was to pay Shs. 5,000/- for a plot and a further Shs. 200/- for advocate's fees for the agreement. A sample agreement was exhibited as exhibit 3. All the money was to be paid to the appellant and a total of Shs. 5,734,946/- was paid to him on behalf of Kimunye by the 16th March, 1982. It was discovered that the appellant had paid only Shs. 800,000/- to Messrs. Waruhiu & Muite under the agreement exhibit 1 and on the 22nd March, 1982, Kimunye instructed the appellant to stop collecting monies on its behalf. The appellant then withdrew from acting for Kimunye and sent a letter to the Company members (exhibit 8) which shows a breakdown of receipts and payments as follows:-

(1) Total amount collected.................. Shs. 5,734,946.00
(2) Payments as follows:-
   (a) Deposit of the first agreement
       for 200 acres   Shs. 300,000.00

   (b) Deposit for the second agreement
       for 70 acres   Shs. 916,000.00

   (c) Further payment in respect of (a) and
       (b) above and for purchase of
       a further 1,000 acres in the
       third agreement   Shs. 2,906,564.40

   (d) Payment on behalf of Gitonga into
       the National Bank (K) Ltd Shs. 800,000.00

   (e) Surveyors to purchase to Town plot
       on behalf of the company Shs. 305,180.00

   (f) Collection charges and the
       legal fees including consultation
       for four years   Shs. 538,315.40

            Total   Shs. 5,760,077.80

According to PW2 Kimani, the only money that was legitimately accounted for by the appellant was the 800,000/- paid to Messrs Waruhiu & Muite and the Shs. 916,000/- paid as deposit on the second agreement. In other words, the appellant accounted for Shs. 1,716,000/- only and failed to account for Shs. 4,018,094/-. It was for theft of this latter amount that the appellant was charged.

Gitonga testified that the only money he received under the agreement exhibit 1 was the deposit of Shs. 300,000/-. In cross examination he said he received some money on account of the second agreement but could not remember if the amount was Shs. 916,000/-. However, it is not in dispute that such was the amount paid under the second agreement.

The investigating officer PW11 Superintendent Kiama produced a large number of documents, many of which were taken from the appellant's possession. He also tendered a statement under inquiry taken from the appellant which was produced without objection.

This statement was adopted by the appellant in his testimony. He referred to the statement and to exhibit 8 and explained the payments set out therein. He pointed out that deposit of Shs. 300,000/- was not taken into account by the prosecution. That amount was paid direct to Gitonga and was not to be paid to Gitonga's Advocate. He paid the deposit of Shs. 916,000/- on the second agreement. Gitonga had acknowledged receipt of Shs. 2,408,564/- in a document which the appellant produced as exhibit D2 (b). It would be as well to interpose there that when this document was put to Gitonga he said that he was there acknowledging receipt of amount paid on an entirely different agreement for the sale of other land to Gakenia Women's Group. The appellant also produced a list of payments made direct to Gitonga between April, 1981 and January, 1982. This list produced, exhibit D26, shows payments of Shs. 498,000/-. When one adds that amount to the Shs. 2,408,560.40 acknowledged by Gitonga one arrives at a figure (all but Shs. 4/-) set out at paragraph 2(c) of exhibit 8. The appellant went on to explain the three further amount referred to in exhibit 8 under paragraph 2(d) to (f) to show how he had dealt with Kimunye's money, and in particular how the amount of Shs. 305,180/- referred to in paragraph 2(e) was made up.

The appellant said that he was the Deputy Mayor of Thika and that Kimani ran against him in the elections.

In cross-examination, the appellant explained that by the time the agreement exhibit 1 expired on the 31st March, 1979, he had not been paid sufficient money by the members of Kimunye to pay the balance under the agreement. He advised his clients about the need to pay such money. There was an agreement (exhibit D14) for the purchase of an additional 1,000 acres. This third agreement was supplementary to the first agreement.

In his statement to police, which he adopted, the appellant had listed difficulties he had encountered in his dealings with Kimunye.

The first point argued on appeal before us was that the charge recites that the money was received by the appellant from the members of Kimunye for the account of the National Bank of Kenya Ltd. It is argued that the appellant was an agent for each member of Kimunye separately but, with respect, there is little force in that argument. There were two types of transaction in connection with the purchase of this plot. Firstly, there was the agreement between Kimunye and Gitonga for the purchase of it. Secondly, there was the agreement between Kimunye and each individual member who paid for a plot on the land. When a member had paid his share the money was paid to the account of Kimunye and the appellant had to account to Kimunye for the total amount paid to him by the members. It is true that the National Bank of Kenya was not the vendor. However it is clear from the evidence that the National Bank was to receive, through its Advocates, Messrs. Waruhiu & Muite, the bulk of the purchase price to pay off a loan to Gitonga. Whilst the charge laid incorrectly stated that the money was to the account of the Bank the appellant could have been in doubt as to what was facing him and no prejudice was occasioned to him by this defect.

The learned advocate for the appellant pointed to various parts of the learned magistrate's judgement which may be open to criticism and particularly that the tenor of the judgement seems to be on civil as opposed to criminal responsibility.

It may be that in this respect the learned magistrate's judgement was not the most carefully worded. Taking the judgement as a whole we do not consider that he lost sight of the fact that this was a criminal trial. In our view he was merely pointing to the appellant's responsibility as the advocate for Kimunye and using that to demonstrate how he could not have fallen down on his duties so badly had he not had criminal intent. The learned magistrate clearly found misappropriation on the part of the appellant, which amounted to a finding of theft.

The other main complaint against the judgement is the reference on page nine therein to the fact that the appellant is the Deputy Mayor of Thika and the statement that the misappropriation may have been due to his election expenses. This was a speculative statement and was inappropriate, but we feel that, as the statement was made after the analysis of the evidence, the statement does not show that the magistrate adopted a wrong approach.

Let us now independently analyse the evidence.

There is no doubt that the appellant received a total of Shs. 5,734,946/- on behalf of Kimunye. There is no doubt that he paid Shs. 800,000/- to Messrs. Waruhiu & Muite Advocates, on account of the first agreement. There is no doubt he paid Shs. 916,000/- as a deposit on the second agreement. Kimani PW2 told the court that the balance was not accounted for and it was for the balance that the appellant was charged and convicted. However, as rightly pointed by the appellant, that did not take account of the initial deposit on the first agreement of Shs. 300,000/-. Nor, after careful perusal of the evidence and documents could Mr. Chunga, for the Republic, argue that the prosecution proved that the appellant did not make a payment to the surveyors of Shs. 305,180/- as stated in paragraph 2(a) of exhibit 8. There is also doubt about the collection charges and legal fees allegedly properly to the appellant of Shs. 538,315.40 as set out in paragraph 2(f) of exhibit 8. However, Mr. Chunga would argue that the balance was proved to have been stolen by the appellant.

We must look to the appellant's explanation for his dealings with the Shs. 2,906,564.40/- as set out in paragraph 2(c) exhibit 8. This does not mean that we are casting any burden of proof upon the appellant. Where money is received by an agent it is possible to discover whether the money has been properly appropriated without reference to the agent. The appellant produced an acknowledgement of receipt signed by Gitonga for Shs. 2,408,560.40 (exhibit D2 (b)). This document was admitted by Gitonga to bear his signature, but his explanation for that document was that he thought he was acknowledging monies paid under a different transaction entered into with Gakenia Women's Group. He is an illiterate. The fact that Gitonga received over Shs. 2 million under a transaction entered into with Gakenia Women's Group was borne out by PW10 Gathaya Mwangi. This was not disputed in cross examination. It is also interesting to note that in exhibit 8 the appellant said that the amount was paid for the purchase of a further 1,000 acres in a third agreement. There was a third agreement exhibited in court but the appellant's Advocate acknowledges that this cannot have been the third agreement referred to in exhibit 8 because the agreement post-dated the letter exhibit 8. Where then is this third agreement? Kimani denied that there was a third agreement/effective and the appellant produced no such agreement. If that amount was paid to Gitonga by the appellant on behalf of Kimunye what was it paid in respect of? Kimani denied that the appellant was instructed to pay monies to Gitonga directly. He pointed to the agreement which states quite clearly that the monies should be paid to Messrs. Waruhiu & Muite. The appellant produced various vouchers showing substantial payments to Gitonga over a period of time, but it seems clear from the evidence that these payments were as a deposit for the second agreement. It was acknowledged by Gitonga in that agreement that he had received Shs. 916,000/-. The fact remains that no land was transferred to Kimunye and the appellant was responsible as the Advocate of Kimunye to ensure that their interests were looked after. Their interests were not looked after by the payment of substantial sums on agreements which were not brought to fruition. The appellant would have the court believe that he was dealing with a difficult client. His advocate would argue that even if he was negligent he was not criminally responsible.

The magistrate found that the appellant's explanation for his disbursement of the money and his actions was so incredible as to defy belief.

Kimani told the Court that when he went to the appellant with his new advocate Mr. Muhia, the appellant said he had paid all the money to the National Bank. That was clearly untrue.

The matter really boils down to credibility. Was it proved that the appellant did not make the payments of over Shs. 2 million to Gitonga as part of a third agreement or otherwise as explained by the appellant? It is true that Gitonga signed a document exhibit D2 (b) which appears to be an acknowledgement of receipt of over Shs. 2.4 million in respect of Kimunye. It is true that Kimani used that acknowledgement in his affidavit to the High Court to stop the sale of the land. However, taking the evidence in its totality, we are satisfied with Gitonga's explanation that he is illiterate and thought he was acknowledging something else. We are also satisfied with Kimani's explanation that he really did not know whether this money had been paid to Gitonga. Gitonga was a defendant in the High Court action, and when he knew of that acknowledging it is not surprising that Kimani used it against Gitonga. There is no suggestion at that stage that there were police inquiries pending or that the appellant was suspect on theft. We are furthermore satisfied that the vouchers for cash signed by Gitonga were towards the Shs. 916,000/- and were not further payments as suggested by the appellant. They cannot have been made under the second agreement because there existed at that agreement a balance of only Shs. 344,000/- whereas over Shs. 2 million was paid. We do not believe that the payments were made under the first agreement because that agreement had already expired by the 31st March, 1979 and in any case payments were to be made to Messrs. Waruhiu & Muite and not to Gitonga direct.

The upshot is that we consider the learned magistrate was right to believe Gitonga and Kimani and disbelieve the appellant. However, the learned magistrate convicted the appellant of theft of Shs. 4,018,946/-.

We are satisfied that it was not proved that he stole the amount of Shs. 300,000/-, Shs. 916,000/-, Shs. 800,000/-, Shs. 305,180/- and Shs. 538,315.40 (see exhibit 8) making a total of Shs. 2,859,495.40. As he received Shs. 5,734,946/- the appellant should have been convicted of theft by agent contrary to Section 283 (c) of the Penal Code of a total of Shs. 2,875,450.60 and we substitute that conviction for the conviction recorded by the learned magistrate.

The appellant was sentenced to five years imprisonment. As this was a deliberate and planned theft of monies entrusted by members of the company to a person in a position of trust we feel that the sentence ought to stand as a deterrant to others.

The appeal is dismissed.

10/10/85

E. OWUOR (MRS)
JUDGE

148

D. SCHOFIELD
<u>JUDGE</u>

ADVOCATES:-

S.M. OTIENO
KEMBI GITURA."

I had always had a problem with my spine, and since I hoped to be released by the High Court I needed not to bother with treatment. I would be treated in freedom. But after my first appeal was dismissed, I decided to make efforts to be taken to the hospital. I had a letter from Dr. Mwinzi, a consultant in nerves. At Kamiti there was a hospital inside the prison, but it was poorly managed and did not have drugs. The prison doctor of the day was a man called Dr. Owino who never bothered about prisoners. He had no time for prisoners. Although we had at least one devoted clinical assistant named Muriuki, he could not do much. For my case, I needed a specialist. I had tried this before but it had become impossible. Since I had not been treated for a long time, it became very serious. My back was really painful at night. However, after prolonged persuasion and insistence, I was taken to Kenyatta National Hospital. We moved by the prison van that used to take prisoners to the Court. The vehicle was normally so crowded that it was even a burden to go to Kenyatta. After we dropped the court prisoners then the sick were moved to Kenyatta hospital. We were dropped at the hospital while the vehicle went back to do other duties in town. I had to walk to the inside of the Kenyatta hospital in handcuffs and under the escort of the two warders, commanded by the corporal. As I walked to the inside of the hospital, I breathed the fresh air of freedom. I looked at the compound around Kenyatta, the casualty department, the family planning clinic. I looked at the women moving to and fro and longed for one. I could pay a million shillings to have one. I thought a miracle would happen but it never happened. Finally I knew it was not possible to have one. In Kamiti it was maximum security and no less. I was taken to physiotherapy department and was booked. As I sat waiting for my turn to do exercises I sat next to a young boy. The young boy had never seen a prisoner in handcuffs. He asked his mother in Kikuyu who I was in irons. The mother told him that "This is one of the thieves who trouble us at night". On hearing that the boy ran away shouting: "I do not want to be near a thief." His mother of course persuaded him to keep calm. When he was seated again I talked to him in Kikuyu. He was amazed. I told him to go and say hello to his father when he goes home. I told him I was a father of children like him but I was in prison. I am sure that boy did not fail to say hello to his father on my behalf on his return home.

I was moved in for exercises, the handcuffs were removed to enable me to do the exercises. Of course the doctor ordered it. There were other patients but like the little one no one dared to be near me except one old man who looked at me and told me in Kiswahili, "Jikaze, mwanaume ni kujikaza", then he told me in Kikuyu, "Ndatuire Manyani miaka mugwanja" meaning in English "Be brave, a man should be brave. I was in Manyani for seven years"

After my exercises, we moved out to wait for the vehicle outside the family planning clinic. It was nice to sit on the grass outside far away from Kamiti Prison. However, I knew it would take long to be out again. The vehicle soon came

150

but it had to go to Kibera to collect more prisoners. I took the opportunity to see Nairobi through the wires. It was a lovely city. I saw many people moving aimlessly in freedom. I envied them and wished they knew how valuable the freedom they took for granted was. I would pay any price for it. We collected the ones in court at Kibera and we proceeded home, our home in Kamiti in our vehicle, the prison van called <u>MARIAMU.</u> As we passed through the streets of Nairobi, I prayed to my God that he should restore my freedom. It was too good to be free. We moved through Kariokor Market. As we passed by, the smell of meat carried by the smoke came right into the vehicle. I felt as if I was eating the meat. I remembered the ribs that I used to enjoy there and now I could not go to Kariokor and have some meat. The smell was so strong that we went a long way before we were free from it. We used to be told that some Luos would eat *ugali* with the smell of a fish being fried but I never believed. I now believed it was possible for if I had *ugali*, I would have eaten it well. We moved fast to Kamiti Prison. As we entered the gates of the prison I thought it was a dream, how did it happen? But we were back home. I felt good for the breath of freedom that I had enjoyed at Kenyatta.

My appointments were never kept at Kamiti Maximum Security Prison. What was important was not the life of the prisoner but the security of the prisoner not to escape. So sickness was not a priority. I kept going to our local dispensary where I got two Panadols when I was lucky.

I will never forget one day I was taken to Kenyatta Hospital. After we were treated, we waited for the vehicle but it did not come. Fortunately or unfortunately, a lorry that was sent by the prison to carry wood came. We were told by the cor-

151

poral that we would go by that lorry. We were still in hand-cuffs. The lorry was going fast. I could not hold on to anything because I was handcuffed. As the lorry moved, I looked like a log inside. I hurt my back, head and my everything. I requested the warders escorting me to undo the handcuffs because I was surely going to die but they refus-ed. The lorry moved to Gikomba to collect the wood. As we waited for it to be loaded, many people surrounded the vehicle to see the prisoners. Some of the children were very curious while some of the grown-ups were really sympathetic.

Some people from home recognised me. They came near the lorry and requested permission to give me a soda. The permission was refused. However, the warders were given sodas. It was very hot indeed and I had not eaten or drunk anything the whole day. As the warders swallowed the sodas I followed it by swallowing saliva. I longed for a Fanta. Surely these people must be very inhuman, just a soda for me and my fellow prisoners. The same warders had already consumed the packed beans and bread that was supposed to be our food. However, I quickly realised that to the warders, prisoners were not human beings. May be that is what they were taught at their college.

Wood was loaded into the lorry and we were part of the load. Nobody considered our wellbeing and our journey from Gikomba to Kamiti was horrible. We were hurt by the wood. We rolled over as we went downhill. The wood fell on us. As we moved fast in the danger of the prison van due to careless driving I prayed to God and swore that if I reached Kamiti alive, I would never go to Kenyatta again. I would rather die inside the prison. Indeed I had terrible spinal pro-blems, but if a patient with spinal problems had to be put at the back of a lorry with his hands handcuffed and rolling all over them it was making it worse. I never went to Kenyatta again.

Chapter Nine

AT THE HIGHEST COURT

In the beginning of October, I was called into the documentation office and informed that the record of my appeal was ready and the appeal would be heard any time. It was a requirement that I be present in the Court of Appeal and that I would be notified in due time. I was not excited because I had doubts as to whether even the Court of Appeal would do justice in my case. But somehow I felt obliged to exhaust the court hierarchy. "Let me go there and see what they will do. After all they will be three judges," I said to myself.

On the first day of the hearing I was present in court, I had engaged Mr. Muthoga to lead Mr. Kembi. Mr. Muthoga did not come and adjournment was applied for on behalf of my lawyer. It was reluctantly granted. On the bench there sat Mr. Justice Platt as Chairman, Mr. Justice Apaloo and Mr. Justice Gachuhi. The three judges looked well prepared to do justice. The new date was set in December and the appeal was to last for two days. After the adjournment, I was led back into the cells. There I found my wife, Gakaya, Mburu and a few other friends who were aware of the appeal. I went back to Kamiti to wait for the hearing.

When I was brought back to the court for hearing, I found that the bench had changed. Mr. Justice Nyarangi was the Chairman while Mr. Justice Platt was now assisting him with Mr. Justice Gachuhi. The court sat to hear the appeal. I was now formally represented by Mr. Muthoga assisted by Mr. Kembi. The state was represented by Mr. Harwood, a senior state counsel in the Attorney General's Chambers who had replaced Mr. Chunga. Later, Mr. Chunga found me in the Civil Registry where I had been left to wait for the court to assemble.

Although Mr. Chunga was a former classmate, he did not even say hello to me! I wanted to say hello to him but I feared he might react negatively to my greetings. If he did and the matter was reported, I would have received a thorough beating on my arrival at Kamiti. That is life, at one time we were classmates equal in every respect but now the relationship between me and Mr. Chunga was that of a prisoner and a Deputy Public Prosecutor. The gap was indeed a chasm.

After the counsel had formally registered themselves, Mr. Harwood did not waste any time, he rose up and told his Lordships that he had a preliminary objection to make. He submitted that the memorandum of appeal did not disclose any point of law as required by the law. As a second appeal, it should only relate to a point or points of law. I had read all the grounds myself and all of them were nothing but points of law. From the beginning, I noted that Mr. Harwood was very hostile. He also became very uncooperative. Maybe he had already known that he had no grounds to oppose my appeal but he had instructions from somewhere to do so.

Mr. Muthoga defended the memorandum of appeal very strongly and the judges came out with an extraordinarily fair ruling. They upheld Mr. Muthoga's arguments and he was to proceed with the appeal. When the proper appeal started, a very important document was missing. This was Exhibit D2 which was an admission by Mr. Gitonga that he had received more than Shs. 2,400,000/- from me. Due to this irregularity, we adjourned again to the following day. The document was then found.

As we proceeded with the appeal, Mr. Harwood continued to interrupt Mr. Muthoga after every five or so minutes. Mr. Muthoga pointed to the judges there was too much interruption from Mr. Harwood. Indeed Mr. Harwood had now become a nuisance to the proceedings. I got especially annoyed because after all it was my fate that was being determined. At the end of the day, it was me Sam Karuga Wandai who would be taken back to Kamiti yet this white man continued to interrupt the proceedings.

As I was going through this agony, it was as if Mr. Justice Nyarangi was reading my mind. I think the bench had also got fed up with the obstructions from Mr. Harwood. At the height of the interruptions, Mr. Justice Nyarangi pushed his seat backwards against the wall, held his lower cheek with his hand and told Mr. Harwood, "We are not happy about these unnecessary interruptions of the proceedings by you. Give Mr. Muthoga a chance to argue his part of the case. We shall give you all the time you will need when you come to make your reply. Justice should be done and we want the members of the public in this court today to go home knowing that justice has not only been done but it has been seen to be done in this court. We want the public to know the legal system works in this court".

Mr. Harwood sat down and from then on he did not interrupt the proceedings again. He kept quiet until Mr. Muthoga had said his piece. As he sat down, I looked at him and I really pitied him. This was a man born in English society, a society where justice is a way of life. He had been educated in the English legal tradition and here he was doing African Justice, "the *kienyeji way*". If he was appearing in the English Court of Appeal, he would definitely have conceded long ago to my appeal because the law was on my side. But perhaps he may not have had the job in England. Judicial jobs were competitive in England and only the best minds are employable there. For those who cannot get jobs to appear in the English courts, they descended on Africa to earn a living. I quickly realised that Mr. Harwood was in a problem. Since he wanted to keep his job, he had to pretend to dance to the tune of his master. I pitied him even more. Concurrently, I now had faith that Mr. Justice Nyarangi was a better legal mind than Mr. Harwood a hundred times and he would contain him. In fact he had already contained him. Somewhere from my inner self, I felt that the judges before me were different from Mrs. Owuor and Justice Schofield and certainly better than Mr. Ombonya. I felt I could trust them with my fate. These men were great men of conscience; they were men of the law. They were no doubt men of great wisdom and above all, these three wise men were men of justice. The appeal proceeded well and I even relaxed and started taking notes. My people who understood English also started relaxing. It was now clear as the case progressed that justice was not only being done, but truly it was appearing to be done.

At the close of the day, Mr. Muthoga came to the dock. He was very happy and asked me, "Samuel" (he always called me Samuel or Mayor), "How are we doing"? I told him very well. He should go on in the same spirit. He had greatly impressed me. He is no doubt one of the greatest legal minds this country has.

Mr. G.B. Kariuki, the then Chairman of the Law Society of Kenya and several other lawyers said hello to me on my way out. My friends also had an opportunity to shake my hand.

At the close of the proceedings, that is after Mr. Harwood

was replied to by my lawyer, it was clear to my lawyers, to my friends in court and to myself that the court was set to do justice. It would even have been better if Mr. Harwood was honest enough to concede to the appeal. I hope one day Kenya's judicial system will mature enough to the extent that state counsels and all prosecutors will be able to say: "I do not support convictions in any criminal or political case which has no merit." At that state, if we shall ever reach it, we shall have come a long way.

The judgement in my case was put on notice. This was in accordance with the traditions of the Court of Appeal. No set date is given for a judgement. When the appellate judges are ready, they notify the parties.

I thought that since the arguments and proceedings were concluded on 18th December 1986, incidentally on my marriage anniversary, the judges would deliver the judgement before Christmas. I felt that since the court appeared so fair, the judges would make sure that I had Christmas with my family. I had a terrible time. Every day I was called to the duty office, I thought I was going home.

As we approached Christmas, some prisoners and myself were awaiting the bread and sugar that we had paid for with our salary. Over Christmas, prisoners were allowed to buy some bread and sugar and some other items to celebrate Christmas. This was the only formal way, save smuggling the items into prison, that a prisoner would break the monotony of the daily routine of *ugali* and porridge. So as we waited and without our knowledge, other prisoners were ordered into their cells and the cells locked. I was in Block A Kamiti Prison then. We continued talking without knowing what was happening. Then the askari who had the count came. Someone told us from the window what was happening.

As we rushed towards our cells, we were met by two warders with their batons. We were about three or four. Each one of us was ordered to pass at his own time. There were two iron doors and as we passed them, one was beaten thoroughly. When my turn came, I was attacked by the two warders who hit me wildly on every part of my body. I was hit on the shoulders, on the ribs, on the back but I managed to hide my head with my hands. My hands were also hit. I was then pushed into my cell. I squatted and the count proceeded. I felt pain all over the body. Somehow, I fell asleep immediately and had a terrible night. It was really a hard night. I wanted to complain, but to whom does one complain? The chain of authority in Kamiti is so interesting that at times a sergeant is more powerful than an officer.

To reach the officer in charge is of course out of question unless one is dying. I perhaps thought the warders wanted to kill me. Surely, it was not part of my prison sentence that I should be physically assaulted by the warders. Beating in prison by warders is so frequent that some people even have their legs broken. This I believe is absolutely illegal and not in accordance with the Prison Act. But prison officers condone it as a normal prison affair.

The new year passed without any news about my judgement. I thought hard; had someone again interfered with the judges? Impossible! Those men appeared beyond interference; in my estimation they could not be bribed. Since the time Mr. Justice Nyarangi reprimanded the state counsel, I was sure that justice would be done. My friends had also witnessed justice being done. So I prayed hard this time.

On Saturday, I was called to the duty office and was told that my judgement would be delivered on 5th January 1987 at 9.00 a.m. When I was told about this, I felt something all over my body. I became excited but I contained myself. I thought perhaps this would be my last weekend in prison. As I moved from the duty office to my cell, I felt confused. Maybe I would never be in prison uniform again after 5th January 1987 and maybe not!

I moved into my cell and told my friends when my judgement would be delivered. They started saying goodbye to me. Some told me I should leave my prison uniform to them, others wanted to have the tooth-brush, even my cloth bag too was wanted. I told them to hold until I was formally released, only then would I be able to share out my personal belongings. Maybe I would not be released at all.

On Sunday, I went to church as usual. Before the mass started, I requested my God in prayer to allow me to regain my freedom. I begged Him to take whatever punishment I had received so far to be sufficient for the sins I had committed in my life. Finally, I asked Him to go right into the judges' heads and bestow them with wisdom and courage to do justice. I requested Him to let me attend the following Sunday mass in freedom and in a free church, "Let me, my Lord, attend the coming Sunday mass in your bountiful freedom."

The service ended and I went to the cell. I played chess with my prisonmates until late at night so that I could gather some sleep. In prison, lights are never put out and one can stay awake until the late hours of the night provided you are not making noise and are at a corner. Darkness therefore becomes a rare commodity.

I could not gather any sleep at all, so I stayed awake the whole night just like the day I came into prison. In the morning, we were called to take porridge as usual. I didn't. I would not die due to missing one day's porridge. Even if I was not finally released, I would take porridge the following day.

The morning of 5th January 1987 looked like any other morning. The sun rose as usual and the prison bells rang as usual. The compound looked the same; high walls on both sides. After those who were going to work had moved to their respective sections, I moved towards the duty office to board the prison van. We entered the van and drove to the Nairobi Law Courts. I was locked in the cells along with other prisoners and when it struck nine o'clock, I was moved to court. As usual, I was guarded by a warder. On arrival at the court, I found that my people had come. Before I entered the court I found my wife with my step-daughter Waiyego on the corridor. I asked for permission from the warder so that I could greet my wife. Permission was granted. I shook hands with both of them as I rushed to court.

On arrival, I found that their lordships were already inside their chambers. Those friends who saw me wished me well. The court was fully packed and was exceedingly tense. People spoke in whispers and could not anticipate what would happen. Most of the people in the court were also there at Kiambu and in the High Court. They had been disappointed twice. They hoped they would not be disappointed a third time.

I was moved into the dock with my escort. Mr. Muthoga came over and wished me good luck. So did Kembi and other lawyers. Mr. Harwood of course did not bother to say hello to me. He could not say hello to a prisoner I suppose because that was below his dignity.

We waited silently, then suddenly the court clerk knocked three times from inside the chambers, the door leading to the court. Everyone stood up including myself. Mr. Justice Nyarangi was still the Chairman. The judges were all well dressed in red with the white cap. They came in led by Mr. Justice Platt. They made the traditional bow and the public did the same. I too had the privilege to bow even as a prisoner.

Now I had reached the end of the road in my search for justice and fairness. What the judges of appeal would decide today would be final. As I was thinking about it, Mr. Justice Nyarangi the chairman said, "Happy New Year". He continued, "My brothers and I have agreed that the decision to which we all have arrived at and agreed will be delivered by our brother Mr. Justice Platt." Then he kept quiet. Platt started reading the judgement.

It read:

> The appellant, Samuel Karuga Wandai was originally charged with the theft of Shs. 4,018,946/- the property of Kimunye Investments Company Limited. This theft was said to be theft by an agent contrary to section 283 (c) of the Penal Code. Apart from the averment that the appellant was the advocate of Kimunye Investments Company Limited, the charge was not clear as to what the terms of the agency were. The charge ends by saying:
>
> > "... stole cash Shs. 4,018,946/- the property of the said M/S. Kimunye Investments Company Limited which had been received by the said for the account of M/S. National Bank of Kenya Limited."
>
> It will be seen that some word or phrase is missing from the charge sheet and that it is not clear what the agency was. Notwithstanding this difficulty, the trial court found that the appellant is guilty as charged and sentenced him to five years imprisonment. On first appeal the charge was found to be defective in that the

money was said to be to the account of the Bank. But the appellant had been in no doubt what charge he was facing, and prejudice had been occasioned. The trial court had 'clearly found misappropriation', which amounted to theft. In the end the decision was as follows:

"The upshot is what we consider the learned magistrate was right to believe Gitonga and Kimani and disbelieve the appellant. However, the learned magistrate convicted the appellant of theft of Shs. 4,018,946/-. We are satisfied that it was proved that he stole the amounts of Shs. 300,000/-, Shs. 800,000/-, Shs. 305,180/- and Shs. 538,315.40 making a total of Shs. 2,859,495/40. As he received Shs. 5,734,946/- the appellant should have been convicted of theft by agent contrary to section 283 (c) of the Penal Code of a total of Shs 2,875,450/60 and we substitute that conviction recorded by the learned magistrate."

It is still not clear what the terms of the agency are. Looking back to the trial court's judgement, the statement of the offence will be found to be:

"It is clear that the accused received the Shs. 731,946/- from Kimunye Investments Company for a particular purpose namely to pay the vendors advocates M/S. Waruhiu & Muite for the purchasers of the piece of land No. 280/3 at Thika before 31/3/79.

. . . .

It must not be forgotten that the intentions of Kimunye Investments Company and the vendor's advocate M/S. Waruhiu and Muite were that the accused will collect the money and pay the vendor before 31/3/79 as expressly set out in the agreement (EX. 1)"

The learned magistrate explained that the subsequent agreements were to be treated separately. So it appears that the High Court had supported the theft by agent of this nature. But that of course does not follow, if the starting point is the collection of Shs. 5,731,946/- and the theft is said to be Shs. 4,081,946/-, when the payments by 31st March, 1979 concerned a part of the payment in a contract, the sale price of which was Shs. 3,800,000/-. The learned magistrate's reasoning is obscure. On the one hand, it was restricted to the first contract for the sale of land dated 21st December 1978, and on the other hand it included the subsequent sale of land, because Shs. 5,731,946/- arose on all the contracts. Nor was it possible for the appellant to have completed by 31st March, 1978, three months after the date of contract. It is therefore of interest to know what the High Court thought what terms of the agency were. That is again a matter of obscurity. It was to be clear to the appellant apparently. That "clarity" is presumably spelt out in the opening words of the appellant's defence.

He said:-

> "I know what charge I am facing. It is for period of 1978 to March, 1982. I was acting for Kimunye Investments who were buying land from one Gitonga Kihara. During this time, I had instructions to collect funds from members of Kimunye Investments Company and put into my account for the purpose of purchasing land. I didn't have any instructions from Kimunye Investments on how I shall disburse the money."

It follows that it is quite obvious that the appellant did not know what charge he would be convicted of, except that he must have thought that he was the agent of Kimunye Investments Company, and there was nothing to do with the National Bank of Kenya. For the National Bank of Kenya was not a party to the sale of 200 acres of land, on 21st December, 1978, by the *eminence grise* of this story Mr. Gitonga, to the Kimunye Investments Company. True, the Bank's lawyers, Waruhiu & Muite & Co., were said to be the lawyers of Gitonga and would receive payment. As far as the contract was concerned, that was on behalf of Gitonga. Why then was it wrong to pay Gitonga direct? Whether Kimunye Investments Company ever gave the appellant direct instructions at this stage to pay only Waruhiu & Muite, on behalf of the Bank is not clear, and indeed would have been a breach of contract with Gitonga, unless the latter agreed also. Where was that specific tripartite contract that the appellant, acting on the instructions of Kimunye, would only pay to the Bank on behalf of Gitonga, and that Gitonga agreed?

The truth was that the charge was anything but clear. This was pointed out during the trial and thrashed aside. It was pointed out on the first appeal and turned aside, it is of this fundamental lack of clarity that the whole case flounders, as will now be seen.

Gitonga had large tracts of land. He had borrowed money from the National Bank of Kenya and was unable to repay the Bank. He started to sell off parcels of land. He sold 200 acres to Kimunye Investments Company on 21st December, 1978. He sold a further 70 acres to the same company on 5th June, 1979. There were further sales intended. Neither the National Bank of Kenya nor Waruhiu & Muite knew of the second sale, at least they are not mentioned at all in that agreement. In the meantime, plots were sold to individual persons, and they collected Shs. 5,734,946/- and had been collected by 22nd March, 1982, when the appellant stopped collecting money from members of Kimunye Investments Company. He gave the following account:-

1. Total amount collected   Shs. 5,734,946/00
2. Payment as follows:
   (a) Deposit of the first agreement for 200 acres   Shs. 300,000/00
   (b) Deposit for the second agreement for 70 acres   Shs. 916,000/00
   (c) Further payment in respect of (a) and (b) above and for purchase of a further 1000 acres in the third agreement   Shs. 2,906,564/40

   (d) Payment on behalf of Gitonga with the National Bank of Kenya Ltd.   Shs. 800,000/00
   (e) Surveyors to purchase of Town plot on behalf of the Company   Shs. 305,180/00
   (f) Collection charges and legal fees including consultation of four years.   Shs. 538,315/40

               TOTAL   Shs. 5,760,077/80

The charge was calculated in this way. Shs. 800,000/- has been paid to Waruhiu & Muite. Shs. 916,000/- had been paid direct to Gitonga. The balance was Shs. 4,018,094/-. That is what he is said to have misappropriated. Once that balance sheet was accepted by the High Court and items (a) Shs. 300,000/-, (e) Shs. 305,180/-, (f) legal fees and Shs. 538,315/40 were also accepted, that is the end of the trial court's judgement. Little could be saved from it.

The case was to be decided against all agreements, and payments on some occasions direct to Gitonga were

166

acceptable. The 'specific purpose' with which the appellant had to comply in disbursing the money was not one specific purpose, but varied from incident, in the first and subsequent contracts. It is the first contract only was in point, the figures should have been restricted. It is also clear that the High Court was more concerned with theft than theft by agent. At any rate there was no one overriding instruction to the appellant on how he was to disburse moneys; Kimunye often gave specific instructions to pay Gitonga direct, and indeed had to pay Gitonga's expenses, despite the Bank. It was only in the final sale agreement that provisions for payment to the Bank were made.

The case now centres on the last item (c) concerning Shs. 2,906,564,40. That sum concerns an acknowledgement of receipt of Shs. 2,408,564/40 by Gitonga up to 28th April, 1981 and Shs. 498,000/- collected up to January, 1982. Gitonga claimed that he had never received those sums.

As to the acknowledgement, it is in the following terms:

28th April, 1981.

Acknowledgement of receipt

I John Gitonga Kihara, do acknowledge the receipt of Shs. 2,408,564/40 (Two million four hundred and eight thousand and five hundred and sixty four shillings and forty cents) from M/S. Karuga Wandai & Co. Advocates on behalf of M/S. Kimunye Investments Company Limited for the sale of my land as per earlier two agreements. This amount however does not include the amount received by me under both agreements signed by me earlier, namely Shs. 916,000/- and Shs. 300,000/- respectively.

I have received the acknowledgements which I agree with and I want to recount and re-add and find out whether the total is correct.

I also dispute acknowledgement number 1 (one) which I say was included in the agreement. Otherwise, I have nothing also to dispute apart from the total arrived at. All vouchers are signed by me and are good.

John Gitonga Kihara

in the presence of
Alfonce Mullu Muia.

(Exhibit D2 (b).,
Gitonga said of the documents:-

"I am illiterate and cannot read. I can recognise my signature. I signed this letter (MFI DI (b) in the presence of Alfonce Mullu Muia dated 28th January, 1981. The contents of letter D2 (b) are correct. The money was from Gakenia but not Kimunye, as acknowledged in this letter."

The main feature of Gitonga's evidence is that he could not recollect how much money he had received from Gakenia Women's Group. He did not know how much he had received from Kimunye Investments Company. He wanted time to take accounts. Indeed Kimunye Investments Company ought to have established how much money he had received before rushing to court.

His plea of illiteracy was accepted by the High Court. It was not dealt with by trial court probably because the acknowledgement was not considered by that court to be relevant. What are the legal implications of the plea? Apparently Gitonga's case was that notwithstanding his signature on the acknowledgement, he had never received the money. Contrasting with that assertion is the statement that the acknowledgement was correct. Against that is the assertion that the money came from the sale of land by Gitonga to Gakenia Women's Group. The High Court held that he thought he was acknowledging monies paid under a different transaction with Gakenia Women's Group, and that the fact was collaborated by Gathaya Mwangi (PW 10).

The attack against this finding is threefold:

(1) that it contravenes sec. 100 of the *Evidence Act* (Cap. 80).
(2) that Gathaya Mwangi did not collaborate Gitonga;
(3) it was used by Kimunye Investments Company to try and save the land from sale by the Bank.

1. Section 100 of the *Evidence Act* (Cap. 80) provides that if the language used in a written instrument is plain and unambiguous and applies to the existing facts accurately, it must be construed according to the plain and existing facts accurately, it must be construed according to the plain and unambiguous language of the instrument itself, and extrinsic words will not be allowed to be given in evidence to show that the words do not apply to the facts. *Sarkar on Evidence* 12th edition page 848 cites *North Eastern Railways vs. Hastings* (1900) A.C. 260 as an illustration of this principle. It was said on P. 263 of the Earl of Halsbury,

> "The words of a written instrument must be construed according to their natural meaning and

it appears to me that no amount of acting by the parties can alter or qualify words which are plain and unambiguous."

Thus, where the words are plain, there is no consideration of what one of the parties may have intended or that the parties may have acted differently.

If that were to apply to this case, then of course, as Mr. Muthoga protested, the court ought not to have listened to any evidence as what Gitonga thought he was signing. As a matter of law extrinsic evidence was inadmissible.

Mr. Harwood submitted that this was not applicable to criminal cases, since the state must certainly be able to prosecute on the basis of fraud or mistake. It was the truth behind the document that mattered.

Both sides may have their respective roles. Sec. 100 is a rule of exclusion of evidence. It puts the best evidence before that court concerning the provisions made by the parties, based on what they reduced to writing. But if a document has not been truly made by a signatory, the *non ost factum* rules may apply. Take *Saunders* Vs. *Anglia Building Society* (1970) 2 ALL er 961. The headnote reads:

> "The plea of *non ost factum* can only rarely be established by a person of full capacity *and although it is not confined to the blind and illiterate* any extension of the scope of the plea be kept within narrow limits. In particular, it is unlikely that the plea would be available to a person who signed a document without informing himself of its meaning.
>
> The burden of establishing a plea on *non ost factum* falls on the party seeking to disown the document and this party must show that in signing the document, he acted with reasonable care" *(underlining ours)*.

There may be circumstances which would allow a signatory to reside from his admitted document of acknowledgement, signed by himself in a criminal case. In this case however, Gitonga does not allege a criminal fraud upon himself. He does not explain how his 'mistake' came about. He does not explain his degree of illiteracy, apart from saying that he can only read his own signature. But this was not his first land transaction. It was signed in the presence of an advocate Mullu Muia. Without fraud, or genuine mistake, or without proving that the document is void, the document stands and if so it must at least create a doubt that the money may have been paid.

But looking at the documents, surely Mr. Gitonga must have understood it. How could paragraphs (2) and (3) have been added, except with Gitonga's consent? The first paragraph is professionally drafted. The second and third are not. It is his case that he needed to reconsider the totals. One can see from the exhibits how paragraphs (2) and (3) came to be added to paragraph (1). The references to Shs. 916,000/- and 300,000/- in the first paragraph could only refer Gitonga's receipts on the two contracts with Kimunye Investments Company. All supporting vouchers were good according to him, a surprising admission for an illiterate. This is a man who owns such property that he can borrow Shs. 3,000,000.00 from a bank. The evidence does not support any confusion with payment from the Gakenia Women's Group.

2. Gathaya Mwangi (PW 10) says quite plainly that the appellant only handed Shs. 555,000/- of the money collected by Gakenia Women's Group. Shs. 2,955,636/- was paid to Gitonga by the Group direct. This does not collaborate Gitonga's denial of payment by the appellant nor explain

Gitonga's alleged mistake as to the transaction involved. If anything, it clearly separates the two transactions.

3. Kimani, on behalf of Kimunye, had used Gitonga's acknowledgement at the stage of trying to prevent the Bank from selling land under its mortgages power of sale. At that stage Kimani apparently believed that payment had been made to Gitonga by the appellant. Later Kimunye disowned such payment. No reason was given for the change, except Gitonga's denial. On the evidence before the High Court, the latter had no justification for allowing Gitonga to resile from his acknowledgement. The burden of proof lay on the prosecution to prove that Gitonga had not received payment, and the issue of payment was highly controversial.

There is no real way of disputing the payment accepted by Gitonga on the vouchers amounting to Shs. 498,000/-. Apart from two, the rest were dated after 28th April, 1981. They therefore arose after the payment of Shs. 916,000/- and the acknowledgement. The High Court thought that they supported the payment of Shs. 916,000/-, that there was no further contract towards which these payments could be made, and in any event could not be made direct to Gitonga. As the payment of Shs. 916,000/- had been accepted prior to the acknowledgement of 28th April, 1981, those vouchers could hardly support that payment. Whether or not the third contract arose, these vouchers could be accommodated in the appellant's fees. While Kimani did start off by saying that the appellant could not pay Gitonga directly, that position was not maintained under cross-examination. Kimani agrees that on many occasions the appellant had been authorised to make payments direct. Indeed the whole price of the contract was paid direct to Gitonga. Kimani said this:-

"I swore that Mr. Gitonga had received more (i.e. Shs. 3,643,564.40)."

"If Gitonga admitted he received the money I would drop the charge."

In the final analysis, it was Gitonga's word against the appellant. Kimani was a by-stander. He could not say of his own knowledge whether the money had been paid or had not been paid. As between Gitonga and the appellant, unless there was evidence of fraud or genuine mistake of which none was recorded, no reasonable court could possibly conclude that the appellant had not paid the money to Gitonga, beyond reasonable doubt. Gitonga was unsure of the payments made to him. He owned great sums of money. He had several transactions going on at one time. He said Kimunye should not have rushed to court without making sure of what had been paid. That is the real lesson in this case. In contrast the appellant has been consistent throughout. In view of the failure of the lower courts to appraise all the evidence generally as well as the evidence and the law regarding the acknowledgement accepted by Gitonga to have been made by him, and in view of the irregularities in the charge, it would be unsafe to support even a conviction of simple theft.

Consequently, the appeal is allowed, the appellant's conviction quashed, sentence set aside, and he is to be set at liberty forthwith unless held for any other lawful cause.

From the word go, it was my judgement! It was well reasoned. As he read, those of my friends who could understand English started smiling. I could not help smiling too. I felt my heart would burst from myself! I was getting very hot all over the body. I was sweating! I held my hands together tightly so as to steady myself. My vision was blurred.

I could not follow the reading any more. It appeared as if I was in the world of a daydream. Finally the golden words came: "The conviction is accordingly quashed, sentence set aside and the appellant is hereby discharged unless for any other lawful cause."

People clapped in the court and there were loud cheers like in a *harambee* meeting. Before the judges rose, Mr. Justice Nyarangi was on it again. "It is unusual for people to clap in court, but since it is New Year, I will forgive you all. Happy New Year including you the appellant". As his eyes rested on me, more cheers and clapping greeted him. It was a very great occasion indeed. The judges moved into their chambers. People then swarmed me. I received a lot of kisses from ladies. They did not mind my dirty smelly prison clothes. Some were crying. I was feeling something in me that I had never felt before in my entire life. I felt a sense of being reborn. I felt in me a deep sense of intense gratification. I felt the process of restoration of my freedom. I felt that at last I was free again. I was not a thief any more but an advocate of the High Court of Kenya. My honour and respect had been restored. I was no longer a prisoner, but Sam Karuga Wandai. All that Ombonya and Mrs. Owuor said about me had been proved wrong. At last, the great judges of the Kenya Court of Appeal had done justice. It was possible to do justice in Kenya after all, hence the vitality of our system. As people continued to congratulate me for regaining my freedom, I could not help shedding tears of joy. I cried loudly to my God for hearing me. I looked around the courtroom for my mother.

I found her. She too like me and others were in tears. Her

tears were genuine. So far she had not known whether I was released and she thought I was crying because I was still a prisoner.

Someone quickly told her the truth. It was Kingaru. She started laughing and crying at the same time. She came to me and as I shook hands with her, I cried all the more. I reminded her of the words she had said to me in Kiambu two years ago. "The God who gave you to me will return you to me." Her God and mine did not let us down.

Chapter Ten

FREEDOM AND AFTER

After the judges left, I was quickly moved to the cells to await transport to Kamiti to finalise the documentation. As I told other prisoners that I was a free man, I cried again. This time for them. I wished I had power to make them free like myself. I could not, but I prayed that one day they too would be free men. As I stayed in the cell waiting for my journey to Kamiti and to my freedom, I felt very genuinely that even if I was to die at that moment, I would die a happy man, an honourable gentleman, for like Brutus, "I too, fear the name of honour more than I fear death."

Since I was born, I had never felt what I felt the day I was set free. I felt a lot of strength in me to do justice and if necessary fight for it. I felt that life was meaningless without freedom. It was only yesterday that I was a nobody in the eyes of society, now I was a normal being. I felt strongly that one should only go to a prison when he has committed a crime. That day I got transformed into a fighter for freedom and human rights. I felt that all have a duty to preserve human dignity. Even now as I write these pages my life will never be the same again. I live a different life from the one I lived before 17th April 1985. I have learnt to live a more realistic and meaningful life. I no longer take life for granted. Moreover, I know the real meaning of freedom.

At about 12.30 p.m., the vehicle to take us to Kamiti was ready. I was still escorted by a warder so that I may not escape. I thought the prison system was ridiculous. I became a free man when I was declared innocent by the court of appeal. However, the primitivity of the prison system could not allow me to be free. We moved fast to Kamiti. I prayed to my God for the vehicle to reach Kamiti safely so that I could go home. I really did not know why I had to go back to Kamiti. It was meant for prisoners and I was no longer a prisoner but a free man.

However, this was not the time to consider all that. In any case I had to go through the unrealistic prison system before I was declared a free man. I moved to my block 'A' and to my cell to collect some few books I had. I met many of my prisoner friends and they were eager to know what had happened. I told them that I had been freed. They were happy. It was very interesting that prisoners should be happy about their fellow prisoner's freedom. Some of them were not quite happy. They asked me, "Who will now be drawing memorandums of appeal for us"? As the prisoners' lawyer, at night and in my place of work, I drew countless memorandums of appeals for them, of course at no charge. I then gave away the few things I possessed including my chessboard with its chessmen. Then I proceeded to my freedom. It was about 3.00 p.m. then, but it looked like morning. It was the beginning of my freedom. As I moved through the prison yard passing by the ghostly looking prisoners under the scorching sun of the Kamiti prison, I felt sorry for them. I moved to the documentation office and gave away the blankets that had to be returned. I also had my salary calculated and after all the deductions for Christmas and other things, I was given Shs. 28/- for the twenty one months I had worked for the state. When I received the money I decided I would use it for a worthy cause. I decided that when I was fully settled and was out of financial problems, it would form the first deposit for a welfare fund for needy cases to be launched by me. I am still very committed to this idea and I also hope that this Shs. 28/- will be supplemented by the sales of this story as I have decided to give part of the money to this fund.

I pocketed the Shs. 28/- and proceeded to the High Office where the commandant and his deputy were waiting for me. I was already in my suit although it was very shaggy after staying in my bag for about two years. This time, I was treated like a VIP. Mr. Lloyd Mugo and other friends of mine had already been to the commanding officer's office, hence my clearance was quite fast.

I moved out of the prison gates escorted by the deputy prison commander, Mr. Ngunjiri and Mr. Muchiri a superintendent of prisons in charge of the metal training section. I was really a great man. That is how our system was like. Only yesterday, these officers had treated me like a half dead man. Today, I was a VIP. Anyway I thanked them for escorting me.

Mr. Ben Muigai had already got inside the prison compound in his nice car to collect me. As I boarded his car, he was the first person to welcome me to freedom. He drove me towards the prison gate and there all my people were waiting for me. My children were there and their mother. They had grown big. They greeted me and I held my Wairimu. She had grown into a big girl. I had left her when she was two, now she was four. Unfortunately, she could not recognise me at all. There were many of my friends, Muriuki, Kihiu, Mwiri, Hiuhu, Gakaya and his wife, Kiiru, Gichuhi and many others. Prayers were said by Ben Kinyanjui who then drove me home from prison with my children and wife. So at last I said goodbye to prison, "a real hell on earth" and joined the free world.

I did not have a home at Thika. My wife had moved to Nairobi with the children. My house had already been rented. So arrangements were made so that I could change my clothes at Lloyd Mugo's house where I also took a shower. After this I was moved to Gikeno which now belonged to my brother-in-law as he had bought it when I was imprisoned.

On reaching Gikeno, I could not believe my eyes. There were so many people that I was really overwhelmed by the hospitality and welcome back home. I was later told that the news of my release had spread like wild fire, so everybody had gathered at Gikeno. But before I was taken into the hotel, I was moved around my ward with loud hooting. It was a moment of great happiness for me. At least, people were accepting me well. I was really moved. Had all these people really come to see me? I could not believe it. The whole bar compound, the entire area around the bar was filled with people who wanted to shake hands with me or just to see me. I felt that the English man was right when he said, "Every dog has its day."

My friends had already organised a goat for me. Meat and drinks were served and speeches made. Kariuki Mbuthia spoke for the Nairobi people. Ben Kinyanjui also organised dinner for me. We went to his house briefly with my wife and several other friends. He gave me Shs. 5,000/- to start me off. This was my first time to see the 200 shillings note. The Town Clerk, Mr. Wamwangi, who is no doubt a very good friend of mine, made the most interesting speech. He said "Every road in Thika led to Gikeno Bar and Restaurant." He said, "I must always consider myself as a son of Thika." Indeed I was a real son of Thika. I was the councillor of the ward in which the hotel was and also an advocate. Actually the Minister of Local Government had not advertised my ward as vacant after my imprisonment. From that day, I decided I would continue to live in Thika; Thika was going to be my home.

We stayed at Gikeno until 5.00 a.m. All my friends remained with me. Dr. (Mrs) Kirika and her husband were there too. She jokingly promised to treat me free of charge until I was free of all the diseases I might have contracted while in prison.

At about 5.00 a.m., I was to go to sleep. I did not have a home to go to. Mr. and Mrs. Waitara agreed to host my wife and I for the night while Mr. and Mrs. Mugo agreed to take care of my children. We went to Waitara's home and were welcomed well. For the first time in twenty one months, I shared a bed with my wife. She still was the last woman I had shared my bed with on the day I was taken to prison.

As Victoria Njeri was to write later in her composition about the happiest day of her life, "Ours was again a family re-united." The composition narrated some of the problems the family had to go through during my absence. It read:

THE HAPPIEST PART OF MY LIFE SO FAR:

It was on Wednesday 17th April 1985 when Dad didn't come back. I wasn't worried because I knew that he had gone to Murang'a. Mum looked sad. I asked her why she was sad, she said she wasn't sad. I didn't bother to ask her again. But that night there came visitors and Mum told us to stay in our bedroom.

The next morning, we went to school and children started telling us how our father was jailed and were making comments that I could not bear. When we went home, I asked Mum whether it was true but she said it wasn't true. So it went on like this and they were making fun of me.

One day, we went to Mama Gaceri's place. They asked me where my father was. I said he was in America because Mum had told us to say he had gone to America whenever we were asked where he was. They started laughing because I had cheated them. I asked them then where our dad was and they said in jail. I felt sad also.

Then one day in July Mum said that we were going to move from Thika to Nairobi. I was very happy because I was not going to be laughed at again. So when we did our exams I was number six because I couldn't concentrate.

On Saturday 10th August we shifted from Thika to Nairobi. First of all, we packed our things into a lorry which was to take our things to Kenyatta National Hospital. Me and my brothers and sisters went to stay at Baba Gaceri's place. We played and had lots of fun there until seven o'clock when Baba Gaceri said that it was time we went to our new home. So we had a long trip in Baba Gaceri's car. We reached Kenyatta National Hospital. We went to a plot called Doctor's mess where we stayed for a long time.

When school opened Mum had problems with schools, she could not find a school for all of us. So she managed to find a school only for me and Irungu then for Muthoni and Kanyoro respectively. Wairimu didn't go to school because she was young so Muthoni used to be taken by Veronica and Kanyoro used to be taken by Mum. Then Mum found out that leaving Wairimu asleep was not good so she used to pay transport for both of them.

Even food Mum had problems. Sometimes we even didn't have enough food to eat because Mum wasn't getting a lot of money. We rarely ate nice food such as rice, chapati, chips etc.

When we were at our new school the language was very new to us, somebody had to talk English so that we could understand. But I also tried to work hard at school, so I became number six when school closed in December.

During the holiday, Irungu and I went to stay with our uncle in Embu. We stayed there for the whole holiday. He bought me nice shoes and Eric was also bought Lawman shoes. Then we came back from our holidays, but earlier than New Year day. We showed mother the gifts we were bought and she felt very happy.

When the New Year came we celebrated it well. That time Mum had plans so that we ate nice food on the new year day. The year ended well and fast for us.

We opened school again in January but this time all of us in the same school except Wairimu. But she also started going to a school just opposite to our school. I was in standard 4, Irungu 3, and Muthoni 1, and Kanyoro Pre-primary. Wairimu was in Nursery. So I used to collect her at lunch time. In school I worked very hard and when we closed our school I was number 5, Irungu was number 1, the others had no numbers.

In April we shifted from Doctor's mess to Sisters' Flats. I was happy because I met most of my friends, and the house was much bigger than the one we were staying in before. And we were staying in No. 81. So we used to play very much with our friends. But when school opened it became dull because I wasn't playing very much. I worked very hard so that I could improve my number but when the school was closed I became number 5 again. In August, we didn't go anywhere because Mum didn't have money for us to go. But she managed to take us to the orphanage where we saw animals of all kinds. We saw Rhinos, Cheetahs, Lions,

Leopards, Jackals etc. When we came in the evening we were bought chips because we couldn't cook food at that time. So we ate each a packet of chips. After that we went to sleep. We didn't go anywhere else but we stayed at home.

When we opened school I started working hard so I felt I was improving and when school closed I became number 3. I was happy because I had improved. So when I told my mother she said I had improved and that she would buy me Sandak shoes. I was bought and I was delighted.

In December we didn't go anywhere. But we celebrated Christmas day although Mum was on morning duty. So we celebrated at night and Mum gave us our gifts. I was given a blouse and skirt, Eric a jacket and a pair of trousers, while Kanyoro, Muthoni and Wairimu had dresses which were the same. So we thanked Mum very much. We celebrated New Year at our uncle's place in Nairobi. We had great fun. Immediately after 12 o'clock struck we started shouting very much and dancing. We ate biscuits, sweets and many things. We loved the celebrations.

It was on Monday when mother woke up and told us that she was going to town to get some visitors. She told us to get dressed very well in our Sunday best. We did so. At 10 o'clock we heard a car coming. It was Baba Waitara's car coming with Mama Wainaina and Mama Patrick and our Mum. They knocked the door and we opened. We greeted the visitors. Then we went to the car and sat in it, but we were told not to go outside.

We started our journey. Before we reached the gate the car stopped moving. So we had to push from there to the gate but still it didn't work. So Mama Wainaina said that may be it didn't have petrol. So Baba Wairimu went to the petrol station which was just near there and came back a few minutes later. When we put it in the car, it started working. So we started our journey to Kiambu, we stopped by a small *duka* where we bought orange juice and cakes.

We went eating these cakes, we reached a hotel where we drank sodas waiting for others to come. After that we went straight to Kamiti Prison where we were not allowed to enter so we waited in the van, then we saw a car coming and behind it were some other cars. Then from the first car we saw the door open and there came Dad. I was very surprised that I could hardly believe it.

But Dad had changed, his hair was cut so I ran to him and greeted him. Since Wairimu was small when we went, she called him uncle not knowing he was her father.

After that we went to Baba Gaceri's place. There we drank sodas, ate bananas and many others.

Dad, Mum and others went to stay at Baba Waitara's place but I stayed at Baba Gaceri's place where I learnt how to cook cakes. The following day I was taken by my mother because she was on duty. So we went and said goodbye to Gaceri, Kawari and Boy. On Sunday Mum told us that Dad would be coming because he had remained at Thika since he came.

So we were very happy and couldn't wait. At about eight o'clock we heard a knock, we opened the door and Baba Wangechi said that Dad had come and he was waiting for us down the stairs. We ran down and saw Dad, and were very happy and stayed up to nine o'clock with Dad because the next day was a school day. We were so happy that now we could work harder at school.

184

We would not go hungry again and many other reasons. And that was the happiest part of my life because I felt as if the world was beginning again.

Other children had this to say about my homecoming:

Chris Kanyoro: I felt like crying because I was very excited. Once I felt as if the world was ending and then I felt as if it was beginning when Dad came home.

Eric Irungu: When Dad came I felt as if I was dreaming.

Susan Wairimu: She was unable to make any comments because she could not recognise me.

Sylvia Muthoni: I felt as if the world was beginning. Now there would be no more sufferings. We all felt as if the world was beginning.

On the day following my release, I moved to my Murang'a country home. I had given up on this home, in fact. It had gone into auction three times, but still it was saved. It reminded me of the old days and I felt very happy. My step brother organised a big party for me at home in Kangema.

The whole location was there. It was a great day for me. My friends Mburu, Mugo, Waitara, Kimani, Kang'ethe were all there. My people from the location, my relatives, everybody was present.

The other party was made in my Murang'a home by my people there. It was very welcoming indeed. In due course, I started meetings as a councillor for Biashara Ward although I was no longer a Deputy Mayor as Mr. Lee Wanjui had already taken over. My certificate as an advocate was also restored in June. The only thing that now remained was to settle down.

As I finish writing this story, I am in my Maboromoko house, while my children are playing outside the house after they have come from Sunday Service. Agnes is watching a cassette on the Video. I am fortunate to have such a loving, committed and loyal family; they are a true source of joy. I have had such dedicated and selfless friends. Precious and priceless friends, I would say. I love my country and Thika more than ever. My desire to serve my country and its people is greater than ever before. Indeed, God has worked miracles in my life like in Ayub's. I am sure He will restore me to the full. I will never stop being grateful to Him. I pray that He will continue to guide me for the rest of my life.

CERTIFICATE OF IMPRISONMENT

KAMITI MAIN PRISON
P.O. BOX 47472
NAIROBI

DATE: 5TH JANUARY, 1987

Prison No. *KAM/379/85/18* Name *SAMUEL*
KARUGA WANDAI

ID Card No. .... was convicted by the *SRMS*
Court *KIAMBU* on *17/4/85*

For:

(a) Failing to pay personal tax for the year ....

....

(b) The criminal offence of *STEALING BY AGENT*
CONTRARY V/SEC 283 OF THE P.C.

(c) G.P.T. cases No. ....

(d) Criminal case No. 1763 .... of *1985*
and sentenced to *5 YEARS IMPRISONMENT AND TO*
REFUND MONEY AFTER SENTENCE IS SERVED

He was admitted to Prison on: *17/4/85*
and was released on: *5/1/87*

Signed:....
Officer in Charge
Kamiti Main Prison.

Duplicate copy to:
The District Commissioner,
P.O. Box ....

....

DATE: *5/1/87*

NO DUPLICATE OF THIS CERTIFICATE WILL BE ISSUED

187

With my mother Njeri

My Kenya Court of Appeal case was heard by the late Hon. Mr. Justice Nyarangi, Rt. Hon. Mr. Justice Gachuhi and Rt. Hon. Mr. Justice Platt, all of the Kenya Court of Appeal. The three judges are made of Justice. Kenya will require judges of this calibre if we are to maintain the rule of law and the independence of judiciary which we all cherish.

The late Hon. Mr. Justice Nyarangi

Rt. Hon. Mr. Justice Gachuhi

Rt. Hon. Mr. Justice Platt